USPAP Reference Manual

Find Answers Quickly to Your USPAP-Related Questions

REFERENCE FOR THE
2020-2022 Uniform Standards of Professional Appraisal Practice (USPAP)

REVIEWED BY
The Appraisal Standards Board (ASB)

APPROVED BY
The Appraiser Qualifications Board (AQB)

ISBN: 978-0-9994241-4-8

All Rights Reserved.
© 2022 The Appraisal Foundation.

The Appraisal Foundation reserves all rights with respect to this material. No part of this publication may be reproduced, duplicated, altered, or otherwise published in electronic or paper means or in any format or form without the express written permission of the publisher.

Table of Contents

Overview 1

SECTION ONE
Guide to USPAP-Related Topics 3

TOPICS APPLICABLE TO GENERAL PRACTICE 4
- **GENERAL TOPICS** 4
  - Acting as an Appraiser 4
  - Advertising 4
  - "Appraisal Report" vs. "appraisal report" vs. "appraisal" vs. "report," etc. 4
  - Errors and Omissions Insurance 5
  - Can This Service Be an Appraisal? 5
  - Complying with USPAP 5
  - Public Trust 6
- **USPAP, LAWS, AND REGULATIONS** 7
  - Laws and Regulations (as defined by USPAP) 7
  - Jurisdictional Exceptions 7
  - Examples of Laws That Can Impact Appraisal Practice 8
  - Requirements Related to Laws 9
- **CONFIDENTIALITY** 9
  - Confidential Information 9
- **FEES** 10
  - The Appraiser Giving a Thing of Value (or Paying a Fee) to Others 10
  - Fees Based on Other Events 11
  - Disclosure of Fees (Requirements) 12
  - Disclosure of Fees (Not required) 12
  - Paying the Appraisal Fee 12
- **COMPETENCY** 12
  - Being Competent 12
  - Lack of Competency 13
  - Geographic Competency 13
  - Disclosing Competency 13
- **PRESENT OR PROSPECTIVE INTEREST AND PRIOR SERVICE** 13
  - Present (Current) or Prospective Interest 13
  - Prior Service 14
  - Disclosing Present (Current) or Prospective Interest 14
  - Disclosing Prior Services 15
- **PRIOR TO AGREEING TO PERFORM AN ASSIGNMENT** 16
  - Predetermined Result 16
  - Unacceptable Assignment Conditions 16

TOPICS TO CONSIDER WHEN AGREEING TO PERFORM AN ASSIGNMENT ... 17

ASSIGNMENTS ... 17
Examples of Assignments ... 17
Physical Segment, Partial Holding, or Fractional Interest ... 17
"Comp Check" ... 18

ASSIGNMENT ELEMENTS ... 18
When They Apply ... 18
What They Are ... 18

APPRAISAL ... 18
Definition ... 18
The Subject of a Real Property Appraisal ... 19
"Subject Property" ... 19
Physical Segment ... 19
The Client ... 19
Appraiser-Client Relationship ... 20
Client's Impact on Value Opinion ... 20

INTENDED USER ... 21
Who the User Is ... 21

INTENDED USE ... 22
Who Determines? ... 22
Identification ... 22
Intended Use and Scope of Work ... 22
Adding Intended Users ... 22
Unintended Uses ... 23

DEFINITION OF VALUE ... 23
"Market Value" ... 23
Source ... 23
Type ... 23

TOPICS RELATED TO AN ASSIGNMENT ... 24

ASSIGNMENT CONDITIONS ... 24
General Examples of Assignment Conditions ... 24
What They Are ... 24
What They Are Not ... 24
Hypothetical Condition ... 25
Extraordinary Assumption ... 26
Unacceptable Assignment Conditions ... 26
Recognize Applicable Assignment Conditions ... 27

SCOPE OF WORK ... 27
Defined ... 27
Who Determines the Scope of Work? ... 27
What Should the Scope of Work Include? ... 27
Who Performs the Scope of Work? ... 27
Who Can Specify the Scope of Work? ... 27
Judging the Acceptability of the Scope of Work ... 28
Same Scope of Work, Different Client ... 28
Examples of Scope of Work ... 28
Limiting the Scope of Work ... 28
The SCOPE OF WORK RULE ... 28

TOPICS THAT RELATE TO APPRAISAL DEVELOPMENT ...29
APPRAISAL DEVELOPMENT ...29
- Assignment Results ...29
- Analysis ...29
- Analyze Prior Listings of the Subject Property ...29
- Analyze Withdrawn or Expired Listings ...30
- Analyze Offers to Purchase ...30
- Analyze Purchase Contract ...30
- Analyze Prior Sales or Transfers ...30
- Analyze "Restrictions" or Encumbrances ...32
- Analyze Supply and Demand ...32
- Comparable Sales ...32
- Data Necessary for Credible Assignment Results ...32
- Exposure Time ...32
- Highest and Best Use ...33
- Marketing Time ...33
- Tools, Methods, Techniques, and Approaches to Value ...33
- Opinion of Value ...34
- Physical Characteristics ...35
- Personal Inspection ...35
- Reasonable Steps ...35
- Relevant Data ...35
- Significant Appraisal Assistance ...36

TOPICS RELATED TO APPRAISAL REPORTING ...37
ASSIGNMENT RESULTS ...37
- "Preliminary Results" ...37
- Without a Resulting Report ...37
- Sharing (or Reusing) Information ...37
- Communicating Assignment Results ...37
- Credible Assignment Results ...37

THE REPORT: HOW TO REPORT ...38
- Reporting and Errors ...38
- Reporting and "Misleading" ...38

THE REPORT: CONTENT ...39
- Applicability ...39
- Approaches to Value ...39
- Client ...40
- Confidential Information ...40
- Copy of an Appraiser's License, Resume, etc. ...40
- Data Input ...40
- Dates ...40
- Information That May or May Not Be Necessary in the Report ...42
- Intended Use ...42
- Intended Users ...42
- Photos ...42
- Reporting the Exclusion of Approaches ...42
- Reporting the Scope of Work ...43
- Source and Definition of Value ...43
- Information That Was Analyzed ...43

    Negative Property Issues 43
    Multiple Opinions of Value 43
    Signature 43
    Significant Appraisal Assistance 44
    Information for Others Who Read the Report 45
    Work Not Done 45

THE REPORT: DRAFT 45
    Draft Reports 45

THE REPORT: FORMS 45
    Forms (in general) 45
    Alternate Valuation Products 45
    Condition and Marketability Reports 45
    Drive-by or Desktop Appraisals 45
    Fannie Mae Form 1004 46
    Fannie Mae Form 1004D 46
    Fannie Mae Form 1004MC 47
    Transmittal Letter (Letter of Transmittal) 47

THE REPORT: RESTRICTED APPRAISAL REPORT 47
    Restricted Appraisal Report 47

THE REPORT: THE DIGITAL OR HARDCOPY 48
    How to Label the Report 48
    Who Owns the Report? 48
    Sample Reports 48
    Security of the Reports 48
    Copy of the Written Report 48
    "True Copy" 49
    Paper Copies 49
    Delivery 49
    Plagiarism 49
    Copyrighting 49
    Words an Appraiser Can Use 50

THE REPORT: THE ORAL REPORT 50
    Workfile 50

THE REPORT: CERTIFICATION 50
    What Does the Certification Apply to? 50
    Who Is Required (or Not Required) to Sign? 50
    Why Is it Required 51
    When a Signed Certification Is Not Required 51
    Content Required 51
    Content Not Required 51
    Content Not Allowed 52
    Signature on the Certification 52
    Date on Certification 52

ISSUES THAT TYPICALLY OCCUR AFTER THE REPORT HAS BEEN DELIVERED 53
    COMPLETION OF AN ASSIGNMENT 53
        Modifying a Report after Completion 53
        Adding Intended Users after Completion 53
        How Long Is the Report Valid for? 53
    THE REPORT: AFTER DELIVERY TO THE CLIENT 53
        Who Owns the Report? 53
        Adding an Intended User 54
        Transferring a Report (which is not allowed) 54
    RECORD KEEPING: GENERAL CONCEPTS 54
        When Selling an Appraisal Firm 54

TOPICS RELATED TO RECORD KEEPING 55
    RECORD KEEPING: THE WORKFILE 55
        Creating a Workfile 55
        Access to the Workfile 55
        Format of the Workfile 55
        Contents of the Workfile 56
        Existence of a Workfile 56
        Custody of a Workfile 56
        Number of Workfiles 57
        Purpose of the Workfile 57
        Retention of the Workfile 57
        Retrieval of the Workfile 58
        Providing Copies of the Workfile 58
        Purging 58
        Disposal or Destroying 58
    SAME PROPERTY, NEW ASSIGNMENT 59
        Confidential Information 59
        When It May or May Not Be a New Assignment 59
        When It Is a New Assignment 59
        "Starting Over" for a New Assignment 60
        Scope of Work for the New Assignment 60
        Client Prohibition on Agreeing to Perform Future Assignment 60
        Level of Detail in New Report 60
    APPRAISAL REVIEW 60
        Geographic Competency 60
        Maintaining a Workfile 60
        Post-Valuation Date Information 60
        "Reading" vs. "Reviewing" an Appraisal Report 61
        Reviewer Communicating with the Appraiser 61
        Which Standards Apply 61

OTHER TOPICS 62
    THE APPRAISAL FIRM 62
        Selling the Appraisal Firm 62
        Buying the Appraisal Firm 62

SECTION TWO
Advisory Opinions Organized by Appraisal Discipline 63

SECTION THREE
FAQ History: Identifying Numbers and Titles 67

    FAQ History: Identifying Numbers and Titles 68

    FAQs: USPAP COMPOSITION, STRUCTURE, AND COMPLIANCE 69

    FAQs: ETHICS RULE – CONDUCT 70

    FAQs: ETHICS RULE – MANAGEMENT 73

    FAQs: ETHICS RULE – CONFIDENTIALITY 75

    FAQs: RECORD KEEPING RULE 77

    FAQs: COMPETENCY RULE 79

    FAQs: JURISDICTIONAL EXCEPTION RULE 80

    FAQs: APPRAISAL DEVELOPMENT – CLIENT ISSUES 81

    FAQs: APPRAISAL DEVELOPMENT – APPRAISAL DATES 83

    FAQs: APPRAISAL DEVELOPMENT – SCOPE OF WORK ISSUES 85

    FAQs: APPRAISAL DEVELOPMENT – EXTRAORDINARY
    ASSUMPTIONS AND HYPOTHETICAL CONDITIONS 90

    FAQs: APPRAISAL DEVELOPMENT – SUBJECT PROPERTY SALES HISTORY 91

    FAQs: APPRAISAL REPORTING – CERTIFICATION AND SIGNATURES 93

    FAQs: APPRAISAL REPORTING – USE AND FORMAT ISSUES 96

    FAQs: APPRAISAL REVIEW 100

    FAQs: OTHER SERVICES 102

Overview

Welcome to the first edition of the *Uniform Standards of Professional Appraisal Practice (USPAP) Reference Manual*. This new publication was designed to help you answer your USPAP questions more quickly and efficiently.

While the current USPAP publication consists of Uniform Standards of Professional Appraisal Practice along with the Appraisal Standards Board's Advisory Opinions (AOs) and Frequently Asked Questions (FAQs), it is not always an appraiser's instinct to check it first when looking to solve an issue related to USPAP. Instead, they might rely on a favorite USPAP instructor or consult other appraisers. That's where the *USPAP Reference Manual* comes in. This manual is designed to provide appraisers with another resource to help navigate USPAP and its guidance material and to easily find the answers to their USPAP related questions.

This reference manual is designed to help you navigate complex USPAP questions by providing you with an organized list of topics. The topics are arranged to follow the typical appraisal process. In other words, issues you would typically encounter before you agree to perform an assignment are at the beginning of the manual and issues you typically encounter after you have completed an appraisal are at the end of the manual.

It is important to note that this reference manual is **not an interpretation** of the Uniform Standards of Professional Appraisal Practice or of the Appraisal Standards Board's AOs and FAQs. Rather, its purpose is to direct you to what may be the most applicable sections in the USPAP publication as you seek to solve your USPAP-related questions as they come up in your day-to-day practice.

> **It is important to note that the wording used in this document intentionally does not replicate USPAP, the AOs, or the FAQs.**

The *USPAP Reference Manual* includes the following sections:

SECTION ONE: Guide to USPAP-Related Topics
SECTION TWO: Advisory Opinions Organized by Appraisal Discipline
SECTION THREE: FAQ History: Identifying Numbers and Titles

We are pleased to be sharing this new product with you and hope that it will assist your daily appraisal practice. If you have any thoughts or comments on how we can continue to improve this new publication, please reach out to The Appraisal Foundation to share your feedback.

Lisa Desmarais
Vice President of Appraisal Issues
The Appraisal Foundation

SECTION ONE
Guide to USPAP-Related Topics

SECTION ONE GUIDE TO USPAP-RELATED TOPICS

TOPICS APPLICABLE TO GENERAL PRACTICE

GENERAL TOPICS

Acting as an Appraiser

A USPAP instructor
When acting as an appraiser in a teaching assignment, the instructor is engaged in appraisal practice and is acting as an appraiser.
FAQ 5, page 189

Appraisal practice
The definition of appraisal practice includes all valuation services performed by an individual who is acting as an appraiser.
DEFINITIONS, page 3, lines 67-72

Services performed as part of appraisal practice
These must all comply with USPAP.
FAQ 5, page 189

Providing a "Condition and Marketability report" is a part of appraisal practice when the individual is providing the service as an appraiser.
FAQ 260, page 298

Claiming one is not "acting as an appraiser"
The individual has an obligation not to misrepresent his or her role; however, it is also very important to understand that most states have laws that require an appraiser to comply with USPAP when engaged in appraisal practice.
FAQ 42, page 205

Publicly identifying oneself as an appraiser
If an appraiser identifies themselves as an appraiser, then he or she should comply with USPAP.
FAQ 117, page 236

Publicly identifying oneself as an appraiser establishes the expectation that a valuation service will be performed in compliance with USPAP.
FAQ 117, page 236

What is a "Supervisor Appraiser"?
This is not defined in USPAP.
FAQ 282, page 307

Advertising

Stating one is "USPAP Certified" in advertising
There is no such credential, therefore, this claim is misleading.
FAQ 43, page 205

"Appraisal Report" vs. "appraisal report" vs. "appraisal" vs. "report," etc.

Appraisal Report
An Appraisal Report is labeled as such.
Standards Rules 2-2(a), 8-2(a), and 10-2(a)

appraisal report
An appraisal report is the communication of an opinion of value.
FAQ 8, page 191

This can be either a written report ("Appraisal Report" or "Restricted Appraisal Report") or an oral report.
DEFINITIONS, page 5, lines 161-162

SECTION ONE GUIDE TO USPAP-RELATED TOPICS

appraisal review report
An appraisal review report does not have to be labeled as such.
STANDARD 4, page 29, lines 868-871

appraisal
An appraisal is an opinion of value.
FAQ 8, page 191

An appraisal is either the act of developing an opinion of value, or the opinion of value itself.
FAQ 8, page 191; DEFINITIONS, page 3, lines 62-66

report
A report has a definition in USPAP.
DEFINITIONS, page 5, lines 161-162

Errors and Omissions Insurance

Is it required?
USPAP does not require it, but a client or a law might.
FAQ 115, page 235

Can This Service Be an Appraisal?

Analysis of Leases
When a client hires an appraiser to analyze leases and the appraiser provides a conclusion of market value, the service is an appraisal.
FAQ 4, page 189

Personal Property Appraiser Giving Value Opinions on "Antiques Roadshow"
Giving an opinion of value, even orally, is an appraisal and the appraiser must comply with all applicable sections of USPAP.
FAQ 6, page 190

Complying with USPAP

Comply by choice
An appraiser can comply by choice.
FAQ 2, page 188

If not required to comply, an appraiser should comply when representing themselves an appraiser.
ETHICS RULE, page 7, lines 176-178

Comply (who must comply)
USPAP does not establish who must comply.
PREAMBLE, page 1, line 35; FAQ 117, page 236

Who must comply.
FAQ 3, page 188

USPAP instructors are subject to USPAP.
FAQ 5, page 189

Comply (who does not have to comply)
An agency can determine that an appraiser is not required to comply, but an appraiser can still choose to comply.
FAQ 124, page 240

Comply (assignments must comply)
USPAP does not establish which assignments must comply.
PREAMBLE, page 1, line 35

Which type of assignments must comply include those required by law, regulation, or agreement.
FAQ 3, page 188; FAQ 4, page 189

Comply (even if there is no fee paid)
USPAP applies regardless of whether there is or is not a fee arrangement.
FAQ 48, page 207

SECTION ONE GUIDE TO USPAP-RELATED TOPICS

Comply by requirement
An appraiser must comply with USPAP when required by law, regulation, or agreement with the client.

PREAMBLE, page 1, lines 35-38; ETHICS RULE, page 7, lines 176-177; FAQ 117, page 236

Some professional membership organizations may require the appraiser member to comply with USPAP.

FAQ 3, page 188

The appraiser can comply by meeting certain obligations for

appraisal practice: An appraiser must meet specific obligations to have complied with USPAP.

PREAMBLE, page 1, lines 38-45

an opinion of value: An appraiser must meet specific obligations when providing an opinion of value to have complied with USPAP.

PREAMBLE, page 2, lines 46-48

an opinion about the quality of another appraiser's work: An appraiser must meet specific obligations when providing an appraisal review.

PREAMBLE, page 2, lines 49-52

opinions that are only one component of a larger assignment: The appraisal and appraisal review opinions must comply with the appropriate standards and RULES and the other types of opinions must comply with the ETHICS, COMPETENCY, and JURISDICTION RULES.

PREAMBLE, page 2, lines 53-57

Comply (which services must comply)
All services performed as a part of appraisal practice must comply with USPAP.

FAQ 5, page 189

Comply with which edition
Which edition is applicable is based on the date of the report, not the effective date of value.

FAQ 1, page 188; FAQ 160, page 256

Comply with USPAP and other valuation standards
If an appraisal complies with USPAP it will not automatically comply with other valuation standards.

FAQ 7, page 190

Comply: how to demonstrate compliance
A workfile preserves evidence of the appraiser's compliance.

FAQ 82, page 222; RECORD KEEPING RULE, page 10, line 277

Complying with USPAP vs. JURISDICTIONAL EXCEPTION
If USPAP exceeds a law, then it is still possible to comply with USPAP.

FAQ 102, page 229; JURISDICTIONAL EXCEPTION, page 15, lines 413-414

An appraiser does not violate USPAP if something is required by USPAP but a law precludes adhering to that section of USPAP.

FAQ 118, page 237; JURISDICTIONAL EXCEPTION, page 15, lines 423-426

Public Trust

What is public trust
It is not defined, but there is context for the term.

FAQ 9, page 191

Who is "the public"?
The public includes the appraiser's client, intended users, other parties who rely on the work of the appraiser and the general public.

FAQ 9, page 191

Promote and maintain public trust
The purpose of USPAP is to promote and maintain public trust through having requirements of appraisers.

FAQ 9, page 191; PREAMBLE, page 1, lines 1-2

SECTION ONE GUIDE TO USPAP-RELATED TOPICS

Promote and preserve public trust
An appraiser must promote and preserve the public trust.   FAQ 73, page 217; ETHICS RULE, page 7, lines 174-175

An appraiser's responsibility to public trust
The appraiser has a responsibility to protect the public trust.   PREAMBLE, page 1, lines 6-7

When buying a firm, protect the public trust.   FAQ 73, page 217; PREAMBLE, page 1, lines 6-7

USPAP, LAWS, AND REGULATIONS

Laws and Regulations (as defined by USPAP)

What are laws?
They are constitutions, legislative and court-made law, and administrative rules and ordinances.   JURISDICTIONAL EXCEPTION, page 15, lines 427-429

What are regulations?
They are rules or orders having legal force, issued by an administrative agency.   SCOPE OF WORK RULE, page 13, lines 380-381

Jurisdictional Exceptions

What is it?
It is a law or regulation that takes away requirements of USPAP.   FAQ 118, page 237; JURISDICTIONAL EXCEPTION, page 15, lines 413-414

For example, a law that requires the fee of the appraisal to be based on the appraised value.   FAQ 119, page 237

For example, the Yellow Book prohibits linking an estimate of market value to a specific exposure time.   FAQ 123, page 239

It is only something that can apply to either a part of parts of USPAP, but it is not when an appraiser is exempt from complying with USPAP.   FAQ 344, page 333

What is it not?
It is not a choice: it either applies or it does not.   FAQ 117, page 236

They are not instructions from a client or an attorney.   JURISDICTIONAL EXCEPTION, page 15, lines 428-429

If a law has a requirement that is less stringent than USPAP, then USPAP could still be complied with.   FAQ 102, page 229; JURISDICTIONAL EXCEPTION, page 15, lines 413-414

Disclosing a client's name to a legal authority is not a jurisdictional exception.   FAQ 54, page 209

It's not, for example, a requirement to use a certain valuation technique.   FAQ 121, page 238; COMPETENCY RULE, page 11, lines 309-310

For example, regulation 49 CFR Part 24 is not a jurisdictional exception.   FAQ 122, page 239; FAQ 124, page 240

For example, when a client requires the use of a hypothetical condition.   FAQ 125, page 240

For example, a client requiring me to give a copy of the report to someone else.   FAQ 126, page 241; ETHICS RULE, Confidentiality, page 9, lines 250 and 252

SECTION ONE GUIDE TO USPAP-RELATED TOPICS

For example, 49 CFR Part 24 requires an appraiser to disregard certain issues related to market conditions, but it is not a jurisdictional exception, and it does not conflict with USPAP.	FAQ 235, page 286
When a law or regulation exceeds USPAP requirements.	FAQ 250, page 294

When does it apply?

The rule applies anytime there is a conflict between the law and USPAP.	FAQ 116, page 236
It might apply if a policy of, for example, a government agency is law or regulation.	FAQ 117, page 236
It applies regardless of intended use, definition of value, type of assignment, etc.	FAQ 120, page 237; JURISDICTIONAL EXCEPTION, page 15, lines 423-429

Who is responsible to determine if it should be used?

The appraiser is responsible, and not the client, intended user or anyone else.	FAQ 116, page 236; FAQ 120, page 238
The appraiser must be aware of any laws or regulations that apply.	COMPETENCY RULE, page 11, lines 309-310

What are the sources of a jurisdictional exception?

They are not clients, or attorneys; they are the actual law or regulation themselves.	FAQ 120, page 237; JURISDICTIONAL EXCEPTION, page 15, lines 413-414

Requirement to identify the law or regulation

The appraiser must not just comply with the law or regulation, the appraiser must identify that specific law or regulation.	FAQ 116, page 236
The law or regulation must be stated and not an attorney's instruction.	FAQ 120, page 237

Requirement to disclose the law

Disclose in the report that part of USPAP that is voided by law.	FAQ 116, page 236

Examples of Laws That Can Impact Appraisal Practice

16 CFR Part 313

This is taken into consideration in the definition of confidential information.	FAQ 69, page 216; DEFINITION of confidential information, page 4, lines 98-101; ETHICS RULE, Confidentiality, page 8, lines 246-247

19 CFR Part 24

This is an assignment condition, when applicable (and it does not create a jurisdictional exception).	FAQ 122, page 239

49 CFR Part 24

The appraiser has the responsibility to determine and perform the scope of work in an appraisal assignment.	FAQ 201, page 271
When it applies, it is an assignment condition.	FAQ 235, page 286

Federal privacy laws

These are addressed in the definition of confidential information.	FAQ 69, page 216; DEFINITION of confidential information, page 4, lines 98-101
When selling an appraisal firm, be aware of the impact of privacy laws and regulations.	FAQ 72, page 217

SECTION ONE GUIDE TO USPAP-RELATED TOPICS

Yellow Book
Prohibits the appraiser from linking an estimate of market value to a specific exposure time.

FAQ 123, page 239

Title XI of FIRREA
An appraiser may have responsibilities under Title XI.

FAQ 140, page 247; AO-25, pages 129-130

Requirements Related to Laws

Those to be aware of
Laws related to confidentiality and privacy.

FAQ 69, page 216; ETHICS RULE, Confidentiality, page 8, lines 246-247

CONFIDENTIALITY

Confidential Information

What it is
Acknowledging a prior service, in certain specific circumstances can be confidential information.

FAQ 58, page 210

16 CFR Part 313 is taken into consideration in the definition of confidential information.

FAQ 69, page 216; DEFINITION of confidential information, page 4, lines 98-101

What it is not
If a written appraisal report is redacted of just the assignment results and the confidential information, the resulting "sample report" is not confidential information.

FAQ 59, page 211

The physical characteristics of a property are not confidential information.

FAQ 75, page 218

When it can be disclosed
When required by law.

FAQ 54, page 209; ETHICS RULE, Confidentiality, page 9, line 252

To whom it can be disclosed (or discussed)
To someone other than the client only when the client gives their authority to do so.

FAQ 55, page 209; ETHICS RULE, Confidentiality, page 9, line 250

Someone that the client authorizes: not someone the appraiser chooses.

FAQ 61, page 212; ETHICS RULE, Confidentiality, page 9, line 250

Only the client, not the intended user, unless the client authorizes as such.

FAQ 63, page 213; ETHICS RULE, Confidentiality, page 9, line 250

Only the client, not a review appraiser, unless the client authorizes as such.

FAQ 64, page 213; ETHICS RULE, Confidentiality, page 9, line 250

State regulatory agencies.

FAQ 64, page 213; ETHICS RULE, Confidentiality, page 9, line 250

Those authorized by law.

FAQ 66, page 214; ETHICS RULE, Confidentiality, page 9, line 252

A sworn peace officer if they qualify as having the authority by law to do so.

FAQ 67, page 214; ETHICS RULE, Confidentiality, page 9, line 252

Peer review committees.

FAQ 68, page 215; ETHICS RULE, Confidentiality, page 9, line 253

SECTION ONE GUIDE TO USPAP-RELATED TOPICS

To a copyright agency but only if the client authorizes such disclosure.	FAQ 71, page 216; ETHICS RULE, Confidentiality, page 9, line 250
To whom it cannot be disclosed	
Data entry services (as one example) if the client did not give their permission.	FAQ 279, page 305
To whom disclosure is not required	
Adverse property conditions do not have to be disclosed to city or county health departments.	FAQ 53, page 209
What cannot be disclosed to others	
Assignment results (which includes just stating the appraised value).	FAQ 56, page 210
Assignment results, even if that person, who is not the client, has a copy of the appraisal report.	FAQ 57, page 210
Assignment results, to an intended user (unless given authority to do so by the client).	FAQ 57, page 210
Confidential information.	FAQ 57, page 210
Confidential information in its own email communication.	FAQ 60, page 212
All details (including the fact that an appraisal was performed) if the client and the appraiser have made this contractual agreement.	FAQ 56, page 210
What can be disclosed to others	
An appraiser can acknowledge to others that an appraisal has been performed.	FAQ 56, page 210
When confidentiality requirements end	
If a client goes out of business, the requirements of confidentiality still exist.	FAQ 70, page 216
USPAP does not have a termination date for confidentiality requirements.	FAQ 70, page 216
Example of complying with confidentiality requirements.	
When selling a firm, an appraiser must comply with confidentiality requirements.	FAQ 72, page 216; ETHICS RULE, Confidentiality, page 8, lines 242-247
How to safeguard it	
By taking reasonable steps (which consists of using sound judgment, taking reasonable steps, and having practical solutions).	FAQ 81, page 221
When disposing of workfiles, take care to not communicate confidential information or assignment results.	FAQ 83, page 222; ETHICS RULE, Confidentiality, page 9, lines 255-256

FEES

The Appraiser Giving a Thing of Value (or Paying a Fee) to Others

Paying a fee to procure an assignment	
This is allowed; however, the appraiser must disclose this fact in the certification.	FAQ 34, page 202; ETHICS RULE, Management, page 8, lines 221-226
Paying a fee to be on "approved appraisers list"	
This is allowed; however, the appraiser must disclose this fact in the certification.	FAQ 36, page 202; ETHICS RULE, Management, page 8, lines 221-226

SECTION ONE GUIDE TO USPAP-RELATED TOPICS

Giving clients prizes or entries into prize drawings
This is allowed. However, this is considered a thing of value, thus the appraiser must disclose this fact in the certification.

FAQ 37, page 203; ETHICS RULE, Management, page 8, lines 221-226

Appraiser not charging a fee
The applicability of USPAP is not affected by the amount of the fee, or lack of a fee.

FAQ 48, page 207; FAQ 49, page 207

Appraiser not charging a fee for a "comp check" assignment
An appraiser can perform a comp check assignment for free.

FAQ 50, page 207; ETHICS RULE, Conduct, page 7, lines 208-212

A "comp check" is not a "thing of value"
A comp check assignment, as it relates to a second assignment which occurs after that, is not considered a "thing of value," rather, it is a prior service.

FAQ 50, page 207; ETHICS RULE, Conduct, page 7, lines 208-212

Fees Based on Other Events

Offering discount coupons on appraisal fees
This is allowed; however, a coupon offering a reduced fee is a "thing of value," therefore, the appraiser must disclose this fact in the certification.

FAQ 35, page 202; ETHICS RULE, Management, page 8, lines 221-226

Reducing the appraisal fee when a "deal falls through"
This is not allowed. Fees cannot be based on the attainment of a stipulated result.

FAQ 38, page 203; ETHICS RULE, Management, page 8, lines 232-234; Certification statements in Standards Rule 2-3(a), 4-3(a), 6-3(a), 8-3(a) or 10-3(a) requirements to state compensation is not based on a subsequent event

Basing the appraisal fee on a percentage of a value conclusion
This is not allowed.

FAQ 39, page 204; ETHICS RULE, Management, page 8, line 231; Certification statements in Standards Rule 2-3(a), 4-3(a), 6-3(a), 8-3(a) or 10-3(a) requirements to state compensation is not based on the amount of the value opinion

Basing the appraisal fee on the appraised value
This is not allowed.

FAQ 40, page 204; ETHICS RULE, Management, page 8, line 231

Basing the appraisal fee on a specific outcome
This is not allowed. The fee cannot be based on a stipulated result.

FAQ 41, page 204; ETHICS RULE, Management, page 8, line 232

Basing the appraisal fee on a pending sale price
This is not prohibited, because the "pending sale price" is considered a factor outside of the appraiser's control.

FAQ 44, page 205

Basing the appraisal fee on volume of business a client orders
This is not prohibited, as it is a client-specific arrangement, so long as the appraiser complies with the Management section of the ETHICS RULE.

FAQ 45, page 206; ETHICS RULE, Management, page 8, lines 220-234

SECTION ONE GUIDE TO USPAP-RELATED TOPICS

Basing the appraisal fee on value, as required by law

If a law requires the fee of the appraisal to be based on the value conclusion, then this is a jurisdictional exception.

FAQ 119, page 237

A client requesting a reciprocal business arrangement

The intent of the request will determine if it is allowed under USPAP or not.

FAQ 47, page 206; ETHICS RULE, Management, page 8, lines 220-234

Comp check assignments which lead to an appraisal assignment

An appraiser can do "comp checks;" however, the appraiser must assure a subsequent appraisal assignment is not based on the result of the comp check.

FAQ 49, page 207; ETHICS RULE, Management, page 8, lines 233-234

Disclosure of Fees (Requirements)

Payment made in the procurement of an assignment

If a payment was made in the procurement of an assignment, this must be disclosed in the certification.

FAQ 46, page 206; ETHICS RULE, Management, page 8, lines 220-226

The appraiser must disclose this fact in the certification.

FAQ 34, page 202; ETHICS RULE, Management, page 8, lines 221-226

Paying a fee to be on "approved appraisers list."

The appraiser must disclose this fact in the certification.

FAQ 36, page 202; ETHICS RULE, Management, page 8, lines 221-226

Giving clients prizes or entries into prize drawings.

Because this is considered a thing of value, thus the appraiser must disclose this fact in the certification.

FAQ 37, page 203; ETHICS RULE, Management, page 8, lines 221-226

Disclosure of Fees (Not required)

Amount of a fee paid

If an appraiser paid a fee to procure an assignment, it is not a requirement that the amount of the fee be disclosed.

FAQ 46, page 206

Paying the Appraisal Fee

Who can pay the fee?

Anyone, including someone who is not a client or intended user.

FAQ 127, page 242

COMPETENCY

Being Competent

When to have it

It is not based on the effective date of the appraisal, rather, it is based on when the appraiser is developing the appraisal.

FAQ 156, page 254

SECTION ONE GUIDE TO USPAP-RELATED TOPICS

Know how to determine the scope of work
Be competent to determine and perform the scope of work necessary. Therefore, if a client is trying to limit the time to complete the appraisal and more time is needed, you may need to turn down the assignment.

FAQ 112, page 233; SCOPE OF WORK RULE, page 11, lines 344-445

Be aware of (and correctly employ) methods and techniques
To complete an assignment, be aware of the correct method and technique to use for that assignment.

FAQ 121, page 238; Standards Rules 1-1(a), 3-1(a), 5-1(a), 7-1(a), 9-1(a)

Taking continuing education classes
USPAP does not directly require continuing education, but continually improving skills is a must.

FAQ 113, page 234; Standards Rule 1-1(a), page 16, lines 447-449; Standards Rule 3-1(a), page 25, lines 758-759; Standards Rule 5-1(a), page 32, lines 1013-1014; Standards Rule 7-1(a), page 42, lines 1324-1325

Lack of Competency

Allowing the appraiser to acquire competency
USPAP allows you to overcome a lack of experience during an assignment.

FAQ 106, page 230; COMPETENCY RULE, page 11, lines 319-325

How to acquire competency
First disclose the lack of knowledge/experience to the client before agreeing to perform the assignment (or during assignment when it is discovered), then take the necessary steps to correct.

FAQ 111, page 233; COMPETENCY RULE, page 11, lines 319-325

Geographic Competency

Have competency to determine the scope of work
An appraiser can realize they do not have geographic competency and need time to gain it.

FAQ 112, page 233

Disclosing Competency

Is this required?
No. An appraiser does not have to disclose if they are competent in a report, only if they were not competent and what they did to remedy that.

FAQ 114, page 235; COMPETENCY RULE, page 11, lines 319-325

PRESENT OR PROSPECTIVE INTEREST AND PRIOR SERVICE

Present (Current) or Prospective Interest

May or may not be a conflict of interest
USPAP does not have a prohibition on agreeing to perform an assignment in any specific situation.

FAQ 14, page 193

Having one may create a bias in the appraiser
Having a present or prospective interest in the property could create a bias in the appraiser, and if it does, the appraiser must not agree to perform the assignment.

FAQ 14, page 193

SECTION ONE GUIDE TO USPAP-RELATED TOPICS

Prior Service

What is a prior "service"?

It is not just appraising.	FAQ 21, page 196
Using a property as a comparable sale that later becomes a subject property, is not a prior service.	FAQ 26, page 198
An appraisal review is a "prior service" of the subject property of a current appraisal assignment.	FAQ 31, page 200; Standards Rule 3-2(c) and (d), page 26, lines 781-801
A prior service can have occurred on the whole property, or just a fractional interest in a property.	FAQ 32, page 200
A "comp check" can be a prior service.	FAQ 50, page 207; ETHICS RULE, Conduct, page 7, lines 208-212

Can a company "perform prior services"?

Only an appraiser is required to disclose having performed prior services.	FAQ 22, page 197

Have never performed a prior service

If an appraiser has never performed a prior service, they are required to disclose even that fact.	FAQ 17, page 194; Standards Rules 2-3, 4-3, 6-3, 8-3, and 10-3 certification statements about prior services

Sample disclosures of no prior services

Sample disclosures are presented in guidance.	FAQ 17, page 194

Can appraise the property again

If an appraiser has appraised a property more than once in the prior three years, USPAP does not prohibit the appraiser from appraising the property again.	FAQ 16, page 194

Cannot appraise the property again

If an appraiser contractually agrees with a client not to appraise the property for another client, that is a business decision of the appraiser.	FAQ 16, page 194

Disclose any prior service from last three years

The "three years" is not based on the effective date of the appraisal but is based on the three years immediately preceding the appraiser agreeing to perform the assignment.	FAQ 19, page 195; ETHICS RULE, Conduct, page 7, lines 211-212

Disclose a prior service, but when it does not need to be reported

When a current assignment is not an appraisal or appraisal review assignment, the appraiser only needs to make an initial disclosure to the client.	FAQ 266, page 301; ETHICS RULE page 8, lines 218-219

Disclosing Present (Current) or Prospective Interest

When they must be disclosed

Prior to agreeing to perform the assignment (or when discovered during the assignment) and in the certification.	FAQ 23, page 197; ETHICS RULE, Conduct, page 7, line 210; Standards Rules 2-3, 4-3, 6-3, 8-3, 10-3 certification statement about present to prospective interests

SECTION ONE GUIDE TO USPAP-RELATED TOPICS

Disclosing Prior Services

What is "disclose"?
It is both informing the client (verbally or in writing) at any time between prior to agreeing to perform the assignment and as soon as it is discovered that a prior service has been performed and stating in the report if any prior service has or has not been performed on the subject in the certification.

FAQ 16, page 194; ETHICS RULE, Conduct, page 7, lines 208-209; Standards Rules 2-3, 4-3, 6-3, 8-3, and 10-3 certification statements about prior services

There is a requirement to disclose a prior service
Disclosing a prior service is required by the ETHICS RULE.

ETHICS RULE, Conduct, page 7, lines 208-212; FAQ 15, page 194

Since a prior service can have occurred on the whole property, or on any fractional interest in a property, an appraiser will need to disclose the prior service.

FAQ 32, page 200; ETHICS RULE, Conduct, page 7, lines 208-212; Standards Rules 2-3, 4-3, 6-3, 8-3, and 10-3 certification statements about prior services

It is not a violation of USPAP to disclose a prior service, rather, it is required.

FAQ 58, page 210; ETHICS RULE, Conduct, page 7, lines 208-212

Who you would disclose the prior service to
Even if an appraiser only works for one client, and the client is likely aware of a prior service, the appraiser is still required to disclose the prior service.

FAQ 20, page 196

The disclosure of prior services applies to the appraiser
It applies to the appraiser, not to the property.

FAQ 31, page 200

It applies to the appraiser, not the appraiser's company.

FAQ 296, page 314

How to make the oral disclosure
There is no prescribed format. It may be appropriate to make the disclosure orally, or in writing. However, when it is made, the disclosure must be documented in the workfile.

FAQ 27, page 198; RECORD KEEPING RULE, page 10, lines 276-278

When not to disclose a prior service
When the client has made it clear that the mere occurrence of an appraisal is confidential information.

FAQ 15, page 194; FAQ 58, page 210; ETHICS RULE, Comment, page 8, lines 213-217

When the standardized form does not include the required disclosure
If a form that an appraiser is required to use in the reporting of the appraisal does not have the correct certification statements, it is still the responsibility of the appraiser to comply with USPAP.

FAQ 24, page 197; Standards Rule 2-3(a), page 23, lines 701-703

The disclosure of a prior service needs to be included when updating an appraisal using a 1004D form.

FAQ 289, page 311

Disclose prior services for each new assignment
The need to disclose a prior service is not just when an appraiser agrees to perform an appraisal, but when an appraiser agrees to perform an assignment.

FAQ 25, page 197

Have performed multiple prior services
Ways to disclose when the appraiser has appraised the property multiple times in the last three years.

FAQ 18, page 195

If two assignments on the property are ordered at the same time, one is a prior service.

FAQ 33, page 201

SECTION ONE GUIDE TO USPAP-RELATED TOPICS

PRIOR TO AGREEING TO PERFORM AN ASSIGNMENT

Predetermined Result

Agreeing to appraise the home for "at least $X"
This is a predetermined result, and it is not allowed.

ETHICS RULE, Management, page 8, lines 227-229; FAQ 10, page 192

Coercion and a predetermined result
An appraiser does not have to certify they have <u>not</u> been coerced to provide a predetermined result.

FAQ 11, page 192

Aiming the value conclusion at the under-contract price
An appraiser cannot select data with the goal of supporting a contract price.

FAQ 28, page 198; ETHICS RULE, Conduct, page 7, lines 185-197; ETHICS RULE, Management, page 8, lines 229-230

A "comp check" cannot serve as a predetermined value
An engagement in a second assignment which occurs after a comp check assignment cannot occur if the engagement is contingent upon developing predetermined results.

FAQ 50, page 207; ETHICS RULE, Conduct, page 7, lines 208-212

Unacceptable Assignment Conditions

Agreeing to appraise the home for "at least $X"
This is a predetermined result, and it is not allowed.

ETHICS RULE, Management, page 8, lines 227-229; FAQ 10, page 192

Nondisclosure of facts
Not disclosing pertinent facts would be misleading.

FAQ 30, page 199; ETHICS, Conduct, page 7, lines 194-197

TOPICS TO CONSIDER WHEN AGREEING TO PERFORM AN ASSIGNMENT

ASSIGNMENTS

Examples of Assignments

Non-appraisal or appraisal review assignments
An assignment can be something other than an appraisal or appraisal review assignment. For example: providing sales data, collecting market data, analyzing reproduction costs, teaching appraisal classes.

FAQ 164, page 258

Appraisal or appraisal review assignments
An assignment can include either an appraisal assignment or an appraisal review assignment.

FAQ 164, page 258

Physical Segment, Partial Holding, or Fractional Interest

Appraising land and only one of the numerous buildings on the lot is allowed
When doing so, do not be misleading about what exists on the property, versus what is being appraised.

FAQ 30, page 199

Allowed to appraise only the improvements?
Yes, as the subject of an assignment may be a physical segment.

FAQ 195, page 268

The subject of a real property appraisal does not have to include all of the physical parts identified as the real estate.

FAQ 195, page 268

The subject of an appraisal can be any or all parts of an improved, or an unimproved parcel, which can be land, improvements on the land, or any other configuration.

FAQ 195, page 268

Be sure to disclose the existence of any parts not being appraised, but that are part of the real property.

FAQ 195, page 268

Allowed to appraise only the land of an improved property?
Yes, as the subject of an assignment may be a physical segment.

FAQ 196, page 269

Examples of a "physical segment"
Any or all parts of an improved or unimproved parcel or tract of identified real estate. Including part of the land, the improvements on the land, a partial interest in the land, part of the land, the fee simple interest, a fully leased, or encumbered property, etc.

FAQ 195, page 268; FAQ 196, page 269

Appraising only a 5-acre parcel of, for example, a 60-acre lot is allowed; however, the assignment may come with additional assignment conditions that the appraiser needs to be aware of.

FAQ 197, page 269; Standards Rule 1-2(e)(v), page 17, line 481

SECTION ONE GUIDE TO USPAP-RELATED TOPICS

"Comp Check"

A comp check is allowed under USPAP
An appraiser can perform a comp check; however, be sure to clarify exactly what is being asked (i.e., is the appraiser "picking the comps" or just "providing data").

FAQ 219, page 279

A new assignment cannot be based on the results of a comp check
A second assignment, for example, an appraisal assignment cannot be based on the results of a first assignment (for example, a "comp check" assignment).

FAQ 49, page 207

A "comp check" is not a "thing of value"
A second assignment which occurs after a "comp check" assignment, is not considered a "thing of value," rather, it is a prior service.

FAQ 50, page 207; ETHICS RULE, Conduct, page 7, lines 208-212

A client wants me to provide them with comps from a neighborhood
To do this and comply with USPAP, it depends on what, exactly the client is asking. If the appraiser is omitting and selecting comparables (they are using judgment), which, in effect, is supplying a range of value, which is an appraisal.

FAQ 218, page 278

If the client only means "send me all the sales in the last year in the whole subdivision," then the appraiser is just supplying data and not applying any judgment to the sales. This is not an appraisal.

FAQ 218, page 278

ASSIGNMENT ELEMENTS

When They Apply

Appraisal assignments
They are listed, by way of example, in the Scope of Work Rule.

FAQ 169, page 259; SCOPE OF WORK RULE, page 13, lines 366-371

Appraisal review assignments
They are not listed in the Scope of Work Rule, but there are those items that are needed to properly identity the appraisal review problem to be solved.

SCOPE OF WORK RULE, page 13, lines 360-361

What They Are

Appraisal assignments
They are listed, by way of example, in the Scope of Work Rule.

FAQ 169, page 259; SCOPE OF WORK RULE, page 13, lines 366-371

Appraisal review assignments
They are not listed in the Scope of Work Rule, but there are those items that are needed to properly identity the appraisal review problem to be solved.

SCOPE OF WORK RULE, page 13, lines 360-361

APPRAISAL

Definition

What is it?
It is an opinion of value (which is distinct from an estimate or a calculation).

FAQ 199, page 270

It is a range of value, including one that is provided by picking the comparables for a subject property.

FAQ 218, page 278

SECTION ONE GUIDE TO USPAP-RELATED TOPICS

If asked to answer the question "Will this diminish the property value?," that is an appraisal.	FAQ 224, page 281
If asked to answer the question "Will the market value of the surrounding properties be less than their current value if "X" happens?," then this is an appraisal.	FAQ 224, page 281

What is it not?

An AVM is not an appraisal. An AVM is an estimate or a calculation: not an opinion of value arrived at by applying judgment and experience.	FAQ 199, page 270

The Subject of a Real Property Appraisal

What is "the subject" of an appraisal?

It is a specific ownership right (or rights) that are identified in real estate.	AO-23, page 122, lines 39-40
If the subject is the "fee simple" interest, there is no USPAP requirement to also appraise a leased fee interest.	FAQ 240, page 289

"Subject Property"

What is it not?

It is not, for example, surveys or studies related to a class of property.	AO-23, page 122, lines 41-46
It is not a type of property, because it does not signify specific ownership rights in identifiable real estate.	AO-23, page 122, lines 43-44

There must be at least one

For there to be an appraisal assignment, there must be a subject property.	AO-13, page 123, lines 45-46

There may be more than one

Appraising multiple properties is allowed; however, that does not make it a "mass appraisal." Mass appraisal is an appraisal method.	FAQ 202, page 271; FAQ 231, page 284

Physical Segment

What is it?

It can take many forms, including land, land and improvements, improvements without the land, or an infinite variety that involve one or more of the physical aspects of real estate.	AO-23, page 122, lines 41-46

The Client

Who can be "the client"?

Someone who engaged the appraiser.	FAQ 128, page 242; DEFINITION of client, page 4, lines 96-97
It's not necessarily the party that "orders" the appraisal.	FAQ 130, page 243
Can be more than one person.	DEFINITION of client, page 4, lines 96-97
Someone who engages the appraiser for a specific assignment.	DEFINITION of client, page 4, lines 96-97

Can the borrower be the client?

If the intended use is for a loan that is related to federally regulated financial institution, the appraiser, per Title XI of FIRREA, is responsible for telling the borrower the lender will need to engage the appraiser directly.	FAQ 140, page 247

SECTION ONE GUIDE TO USPAP-RELATED TOPICS

The client vs. the intended user
An intended user does not have an appraiser-client relationship.

FAQ 128, page 242; DEFINITION of intended user, page 4, lines 127-128

Who can "act" as the client?
The client can hire an agent to act on their behalf.

FAQ 129, page 242; DEFINITION of client, page 4, lines 96-97

For example, an appraisal management company (AMC) can be an agent acting on the client's behalf.

FAQ 129, page 242; DEFINITION of client, page 4, lines 96-97

Someone can act on a client's behalf, but the appraiser must be able to identify the client.

FAQ 131, page 243; Standards Rule 1-2(a), page 16, lines 459; Standards Rule 3-2(a), page 25, line 775), Standards Rule 5-2(a), page 33, line 1022; Standards Rule 7-2(a), page 42, line 1335; Standards Rule 9-2(a), page 51, line 1662

Can an AMC be the client?
If the client hired an agent to act on their behalf, such as an AMC, that does not make the AMC the client.

FAQ 129, page 242; DEFINITION of client, page 4, lines 96-97

Anyone can be a client, including an AMC. If the AMC is not acting as an agent, but is the one who engages the appraiser on their own behalf, then they are the client.

FAQ 130, page 243

Identity of the client
The appraiser must know the identity of the client, even if an agent is acting on their behalf.

FAQ 131, page 243

Appraiser-Client Relationship

When it ends
Never. USPAP does not provide a provision for the termination of the relationship.

FAQ 70, page 216

If a client goes out of business, the requirements of confidentiality still exist.

FAQ 70, page 216

Who has it?
For appraisals already completed: an appraiser selling an appraisal firm has the relationship, not the appraiser buying the firm.

FAQ 72, page 216; FAQ 73, page 217

When it can be replaced with another party
Never. Changing the client's name on a report is misleading.

FAQ 133, page 244

Client's Impact on Value Opinion

No impact
All else being the same in an appraisal or appraisal review assignment, the type of client would have no impact on the appraiser's value opinion.

FAQ 169, page 259; ETHICS RULE, Management, page 8, line 230; ETHICS RULE, Conduct, page 7, lines 185-186

INTENDED USER

Who the User Is

Who can be the "intended user"?
The client is always an intended user.
FAQ 128, page 242; DEFINITION of intended user, page 4, lines 127-128

Who it might not be
In a lending assignment, a borrower is not typically an intended user.
FAQ 138, page 246; Standards Rule 2-2(a)(ii)

Identifying the intended user
The appraiser is responsible for identifying the intended user.
FAQ 135, page 244

The appraiser must identify the intended user.
FAQ 137, page 246; SCOPE OF WORK RULE, page 13, lines 360-361, 366

No one is "automatically" an intended user except the client.
FAQ 135, page 244; DEFINITION of intended user, page 4, lines 127-128

The intended user is not established by who may or may not receive a copy or use a copy of a report.
FAQ 135, page 244

Even if a law or regulation requires a party to receive a copy of the report, this does not make them an intended user.
FAQ 135, page 244; Standards Rule 2-2(ii), comment, page 20, lines 597-599; Standards Rule 8-2(a)(i), Comment, page 46, lines 1482-1484; Standards Rule 10-2(a)(ii), comment, page 54, lines 1773-1774

Stating the identity of the intended user
The identity of the intended user must be stated in the report, even if the client is the only intended user.
FAQ 136, page 245

In an Appraisal Report, the intended user must be identified by name or type.
FAQ 136, page 245; Standards Rule 2-2(a)(ii)

In a Restricted Appraisal Report, the intended user must be identified by name.
FAQ 136, page 245; Standards Rule 2-2(b)(ii)

Intended users can be identified by type, but only for an Appraisal Report.
FAQ 139, page 247; Standards Rule 2-2(a)

When to not state the identity of an intended user
When the client is the only intended user and has requested anonymity.
FAQ 136, page 245; ETHICS RULE, Confidentiality, page 9, lines 248-254

"Adding" an intended user
An intended user must be known at the time of the assignment, and not later.
FAQ 132, page 243; DEFINITION of intended user, page 4, lines 127-128

After the report is delivered to the client, an intended user cannot be added to the report.
FAQ 132, page 243

Multiple intended users
Are allowed.
FAQ 139, page 247; FAQ 187, page 266

SECTION ONE GUIDE TO USPAP-RELATED TOPICS

Knowing but not stating the identity of an intended user in a report
Is not allowed for a Restricted Appraisal Report. — FAQ 139, page 247

Is allowed for an Appraisal Report, so long as the intended user is identified by type. — FAQ 139, page 247

A subsequent user vs. an intended user
A subsequent user is not defined in USPAP and is not an intended user. — FAQ 132, page 243

Rights of intended users
A client can give an intended user a copy of a Restricted Appraisal Report. — FAQ 305, page 318

INTENDED USE

Who Determines?

The client
The determination of the intended use is related to the client's use. — FAQ 135, page 245

Obligations of the appraiser
If a borrower seeking to apply for a loan wants to use the appraisal in conjunction with a federally related transaction, the appraiser would need to inform the potential client (the future borrower) that they may not be able to use the appraisal for that purpose. — FAQ 140, page 247; AO-25, pages 129-130

Identification

Who identifies the intended use?
The appraiser, in the problem identification, identifies the intended use. — FAQ 137, page 246; Standards Rule 1-2

When to determine the intended user
At the time of the assignment; however, there is a scenario where an intended user can be identified during the assignment and it does not trigger a new assignment. — FAQ 145, page 249

Intended Use and Scope of Work

Why it matters
During the assignment, it is what determines the appropriate scope of work. — FAQ 135, page 245

During the assignment, it is what helps determine the appropriate type of report. — FAQ 135, page 245

Adding Intended Users

New assignment
Yes, if adding an intended user during the assignment results in a change in the scope of work. — FAQ 145, page 249

Allowed
Not after the assignment has been **delivered to the client**. — FAQ 145, page 249; DEFINITION of intended user, page 4, lines 127-128

Yes, so long as it is **during** the assignment. — FAQ 145, page 249

The appraiser can opt to call it a new assignment if they want (even if it does not need, per USPAP, be a new assignment). — FAQ 145, page 249

Unintended Uses

Parties who receive a copy of the report
The appraiser cannot know what decisions another party is trying to make about value, so it would be impossible for an appraiser to develop and report an appraisal that can address the knowledge needs of some unknown person.

FAQ 135, page 245

DEFINITION OF VALUE

"Market Value"

The definition in USPAP
USPAP does not provide a specific definition of "value."

FAQ 176, page 262

The definition in USPAP contains the components a definition of "market value" would have. If, in other words, the USPAP "definition" of market value is not one that could be cited to meet the requirement to identify and state the definition of value.

DEFINITION of market value, page 5, lines 131-135

The USPAP definition of value contains a list of the specific characteristics and conditions needed to be identified to qualify as a type of value that is considered a "market value" definition.

FAQ 176, page 262

Source

What sources are acceptable?
USPAP does not endorse any particular source, but sources would include a regulatory agency, a legal jurisdiction, an engagement letter, or a textbook.

FAQ 176, page 262

An engagement letter is an acceptable source for the type and definition of value.

FAQ 178, page 263

Type

What is a "type" of value?
It is a general class or category of value, such as market value, fair value, etc.

FAQ 176, page 262

For example, "value in use" is a type of value and the appraiser may use this as a type of value for the assignment.

FAQ 188, page 266

SECTION ONE GUIDE TO USPAP-RELATED TOPICS

TOPICS RELATED TO AN ASSIGNMENT

ASSIGNMENT CONDITIONS

General Examples of Assignment Conditions

Laws and regulations
Those related to confidentiality and privacy laws.
FAQ 69, page 216; ETHICS RULE, Confidentiality, page 8, lines 246-247

Those conditions that are required by some users of appraisal services
Such as those assignment conditions required by federally regulated financial institutions.
FAQ 130, page 243

Those conditions required by Fannie Mae
This includes assignment conditions about the treatment of seller concessions in an appraisal.
FAQ 179, page 263

Fannie Mae, or others, may place limits on the size of adjustments.
FAQ 211, page 276

Measuring a home using ANSI standards
This is not required by USPAP, but it may be an assignment condition.
FAQ 181, page 264

Minimum number of comparable sales
A client may require a minimum number of comparable sales; however, USPAP does not have such a requirement.
FAQ 249, page 294

Analyses of the listing history of the subject property
A client may require the appraiser to analyze and report on any listing history.
FAQ 255, page 296

What They Are

Definition
They would affect the scope of work.
FAQ 146, page 294; DEFINITION of assignment conditions, page 3, lines 81-82

Examples include:
"The appraiser must develop two approaches to value."
FAQ 146, page 249

"Appraise the property using plans and specifications."
FAQ 146, page 249

"The report must include as-is market value."
FAQ 146, page 249

What They Are Not

Client conditions.
Client conditions do not affect the scope of work but are part of an appraiser's assignment.
FAQ 146, page 249

Examples of client conditions include:

"The report must include photographs of the street." FAQ 146, page 249

"The report must be emailed." FAQ 146, page 249

Turn times or due dates.

Are not assignment conditions, they are contractual obligations. FAQ 225, page 281

Hypothetical Condition

Definition
Something that is contrary to what is known. FAQ 125, page 240; FAQ 232, page 285; DEFINITIONS, page 4, lines 117-121

Examples
Appraising a property with a different zoning, etc. FAQ 233, page 285

Appraising a property as it if had a covenant in place, when in fact it does not. FAQ 239, page 288

When one can be used
Only if the use of one is for legal purposes, purposes of reasonable analysis or purposes of comparison, and if the use of one results in a credible analysis. FAQ 234, page 286

Is it the same as a jurisdictional exception?
No. Thus, the use of one is not an example of applying the JURISDICTIONAL EXCEPTION RULE. FAQ 124, page 240

As it relates to new construction
May be used if the opinion of value is a current effective date, and the appraisal is being done as if the construction were already complete. FAQ 154, page 253; Standards Rule 1-2(g), page 17, lines 497-501

May not be used (instead, an extraordinary assumption should be used) if the opinion of value is based on a future date. FAQ 154, page 253; Standards Rule 1-2(f), page 17, lines 492-496

Not required if the assignment is to value the property as-is and not as-if-completed as of the current date. FAQ 237, page 288

As it relates to appraising only a physical segment
A hypothetical condition may or may not be necessary. FAQ 195, page 268

Is likely not necessary when appraising only the underlying land of an improved property. FAQ 196, page 269

When appraising two lots as if they are one
If two lots exist as two legally separate lots, but the lender wants them appraised as one lot, this is a hypothetical condition. FAQ 223, page 280

Reporting
The appraiser is to report any hypothetical conditions used and that their use may have affected assignment results. FAQ 236, page 287; Standards Rules 2-1(c), page 578-579, 2-2(a)(xiii), page 22, lines 637-639

Be clear and conspicuous when reporting hypothetical conditions. FAQ 236, page 287; Standards Rule 2-2(a)(xiii), page 22, line 637

Clearly and accurately disclose all hypothetical conditions. FAQ 236, page 287

SECTION ONE GUIDE TO USPAP-RELATED TOPICS

Extraordinary Assumption

Definition
Something that is uncertain.	FAQ 232, page 285; DEFINITIONS, page 4, lines 111-115
If an appraiser cannot confirm facts (and it is appropriate to use the extraordinary assumptions).	FAQ 241, page 289

Examples of when to use
Appraising proposed improvements as of the date of completion, etc.	FAQ 232, page 285
If an appraiser cannot confirm something that is uncertain, such as the existence of an easement that is not recorded.	FAQ 241, page 289
If an appraiser receives property information from someone else, the appraiser has to determine if an extraordinary assumption about the information is appropriate or not.	FAQ 243, page 290; AO-2, lines 76-86, page 69

As it relates to proposed new construction
May be used if the opinion of value is a prospective date.	FAQ 154, page 253; Standards Rule 1-2(f), page 17, lines 492-496
Use an extraordinary assumption for proposed new construction if the assumption is the property will be complete in the future.	FAQ 242, page 290

As it relates to appraising only a physical segment
An extraordinary assumption may or may not be necessary.	FAQ 195, page 268
Is likely not necessary when appraising only the underlying land of an improved property.	FAQ 196, page 269

Reporting
The appraiser is to report any extraordinary assumptions used and that their use may have affected assignment results.	FAQ 236, page 287; Standards Rules 2-1(c), page 20, lines 578-579, 2-2(a)(xiii), page 21 lines 616-618
Be clear and conspicuous when reporting extraordinary assumptions.	FAQ 236, page 287; Standards Rule 2-2(a)(xiii), line 637
Clearly and accurately disclose all extraordinary assumptions.	FAQ 236, page 287; Standards Rule 2-1(c), lines 578-579

Labeling
USPAP does not require an extraordinary assumption to be labeled as such (or for the specific term "extraordinary assumption" to be used).	FAQ 237, page 288

Unacceptable Assignment Conditions

Too short of a turnaround time
If the turnaround time is too short to complete the appropriate scope of work, this is an unacceptable assignment condition.	FAQ 112, page 233; SCOPE OF WORK RULE, page 14, lines 392-393

Client's request to disregard relevant comparables
Is not allowed. The appraiser must analyze comparable sales data.	FAQ 144, page 248; Standards Rule 1-4(a), page 18 lines 520-521

The client making the scope of work decision
Is not allowed. The appraiser must make both the decision as to what the appropriate scope of work would be and the appraiser must also perform the scope of work.	FAQ 168, page 259

Recognize Applicable Assignment Conditions

Failure to do so
Would be a violation of the ETHICS RULE or COMPETENCY RULE.

FAQ 197, page 269

SCOPE OF WORK

Defined

What is it?
It is the work the appraiser performs to develop assignment results.

FAQ 163, page 258

As defined, it is the type and extent of research and analysis in an appraisal or appraisal review assignment.

FAQ 163, page 258; DEFINITION of scope of work, page 5, line 163

What is it not?
It is not reporting.

FAQ 163, page 258; DEFINITION of scope of work, page 5, line 163

Who Determines the Scope of Work?

The appraiser
Only the appraiser can determine the appropriate scope of work.

FAQ 165, page 258; SCOPE OF WORK RULE, page 13, lines 347-349

What Should the Scope of Work Include?

Interior inspection
An interior inspection is not required. It is the appraiser's responsibility to determine the appropriate scope of work, including the degree of inspection necessary to produce credible assignment results.

FAQ 189, page 266; AO-2, page 69, lines 46 and 50-52

An interior inspection should be made if the act of not conducting one would result in a substantial error of omission or commission that significantly affects an appraisal.

FAQ 190, page 267

If adequate information is not available about a property, the appraiser, who controls the scope of work, will either need to withdraw from the assignment, expand the scope of work to gather that information, or use an extraordinary assumption.

FAQ 190, page 267

Who Performs the Scope of Work?

The appraiser
Only the appraiser can perform the scope of work.

FAQ 164, page 258

Who Can Specify the Scope of Work?

The client
The client can specify the scope of work; however, the appraiser must approve it as one that will allow the appraiser to develop credible assignment results.

FAQ 166, page 258

Judging the Acceptability of the Scope of Work

Appraiser's peers

An appraiser must know what his or her peers would do for a similar assignment.	**FAQ 175, page 262; DEFINITION** of appraiser's peers, page 3, line 79
The "appraiser's peers" are assignment specific.	**FAQ 175, page 262; DEFINITION** of appraiser's peers, page 3, line 79
Knowledge about what an appraiser's peers would do comes from being a participant in the profession.	**FAQ 175, page 262**

Same Scope of Work, Different Client

Does the client impact the value conclusion?

If the scope of work and the assignment elements are identical, the client would not impact the appraiser's value conclusion.	**FAQ 169, page 259**

Examples of Scope of Work

Inspecting photos of a property (is that a personal inspection)?

No. Thus, the appraiser cannot indicate, in the certification, that they personally inspected the property, if they only inspected photos of the property.	**FAQ 191, page 267**

Using MLS photos in a report

Depending on what scope of work is appropriate for the assignment, this either will or will not be ok.	**FAQ 192, page 268**

For proposed construction

An appraiser does not have to review, specifically, plans and specifications, they can view "other documentation sufficient to identify the extent and character of the proposed improvements."	**FAQ 198, page 270; Standards Rule 1-2(e)(i)-(v)**

Limiting the Scope of Work

Limiting scope of work to a "new client name"

Is not allowed. In this instance, the client would be the one who made the scope of work decision.	**FAQ 168, page 259**

The SCOPE OF WORK RULE

When does it apply?

It only applies to appraisal or appraisal review assignments.	**FAQ 164, page 258**
Examples of assignments where it would not apply include teaching appraisal courses, providing sales data, collecting market data, analyzing reproduction costs, developing educational textbooks.	**FAQ 164, page 258**

TOPICS THAT RELATE TO APPRAISAL DEVELOPMENT

APPRAISAL DEVELOPMENT

Assignment Results

What they are
Examples include identifying "functional problems" or "the interior is dated."

FAQ 76, page 218

What they are not
Physical characteristics are not assignment results.

FAQ 75, page 218

Examples of things that are not assignment results: property address, year of construction, number of bedrooms.

FAQ 76, page 218; FAQ 77, page 219; FAQ 78, page 219; FAQ 79, page 220; FAQ 80, page 220

Who they can be communicated to
For one example: state regulatory agencies.

FAQ 65, page 214; ETHICS RULE, Confidentiality, page 9, line 251

Analysis

What is it?
"Analysis" is not defined in USPAP and thus, the common English language definition from any common dictionary applies.

FAQ 256, page 296

Proper analysis, therefore, is a scope of work decision.

FAQ 256, page 296

The acceptability of the analysis will then be judged in the same way that any other scope of work decision is judged.

FAQ 256, page 296; SCOPE OF WORK ACCEPTABILITY, page 14, lines 382-401; AO-28, pages 136-139; AO-29, pages 140-141

When to perform an analysis
If an analysis of some specific information is not necessary for credible assignment results, then the analysis is not required to be performed or reported.

FAQ 262, page 299; FAQ 263, page 299; Standards Rule 7-5(a), page 45, lines 1440-1444

Analyze Prior Listings of the Subject Property

When is this required?
USPAP does not require, specifically, that prior listings be analyzed. However, if the lack of analyzing the information results in committing a substantial error of omission or commission that significantly affects an appraisal, then those analyses should be completed.

FAQ 255, page 296; Standards Rule 1-1(b), page 16, line 450

When it is an assignment condition.

FAQ 255, page 296

SECTION ONE GUIDE TO USPAP-RELATED TOPICS

Analyze Withdrawn or Expired Listings

Listings which have expired

Are not required to be considered or analyzed, unless excluding that information would result in a substantial error of omission or commission.

FAQ 258, page 297; Standards Rule 1-1(b), page 16, line 450

Analyze Offers to Purchase

Offers made prior to the effective date of the appraisal

Are not required to be considered or analyzed, unless excluding that information would result in a substantial error of omission or commission.

FAQ 246, page 293; Standards Rule 1-5(a), page 19, lines 555-559; Standards Rule 1-1(b), page 16, line 450

Analyze Purchase Contract

How, if it is not provided?

If the contract is available to the appraiser, it must be analyzed.

FAQ 208, page 275; Standards Rule 1-5, page 19, lines 555-559

The appraiser has an obligation to make an effort to obtain a copy of the purchase contract.

FAQ 208, page 275; FAQ 209, page 275; Standards Rule 1-5(a)

If a copy of the contract is withheld intentionally, the appraiser can still complete the assignment but must disclose what efforts were made to obtain the contract.

FAQ 247, page 293; Standards Rule 1-5, page 19, lines 556-557; Standards Rules 2-2(a)(x)(3), page 21, lines 627-629 and 2-2(b)(xii)(3), 8-2(a)(x)(3) and 8-2(b)(xii); AO-24, pages 126-128

How, if the purchase price is withheld from the appraiser?

The appraiser is not required to know the agreed upon sale price. The appraiser can still complete the assignment but must disclose the scope of work that was applicable for this assignment.

FAQ 252, page 295; Standards Rule 1-5(a), page 19, lines 556-557; AO-24, pages 126-128

What does it mean to perform a "proper analysis"?

"Analysis" is not defined in USPAP and thus, the common English language definition from any common dictionary applies.

FAQ 256, page 296

Proper analysis, therefore, is a scope of work decision.

FAQ 256, page 296

The acceptability of the analysis will then be judged in the same way that any other scope of work decision is judged.

FAQ 256, page 296; SCOPE OF WORK ACCEPTABILITY, page 14, lines 382-401; AO-28, pages 136-139; AO-29, pages 140-141

Relationship of sale price and appraised value

An appraiser is not engaged to support contract prices. The sales price and the appraised value may or may not relate to one another.

FAQ 257, page 297

Analyze Prior Sales or Transfers

When this analysis is not specifically required

When the appraiser is not performing a real property appraisal. STANDARD 1 only applies to appraisal and appraisal review assignments.

FAQ 260, page 298

If the analysis is not necessary for credible assignment results.

FAQ 262, page 299; FAQ 251, page 295 and FAQ 263, page 299; Standards Rule 7-5(a), page 45, lines 1440-1443

What is being analyzed?	
The prior sale of the subject property, including a sale of a portion of the subject property that sold.	FAQ 264, page 299; Standards Rule 9-4(b)(vi), page 53, lines 1718-1719
What is considered a "sale"?	
For example, a deed in lieu of foreclosure is a sale.	FAQ 254, page 296; Standards Rule 1-5(b), page 19, lines 560-561
Multiple sales or transfers	
The appraiser must analyze any and all types of sale in the past three years, not just the most recent one.	FAQ 245, page 292; Standards Rule 1-5, page 19, lines 555-561; Standards Rule 2-2(a)(x)(3), page 21, lines 625-629; AO-1, page 65-67
What to disclose when there has only been one sale	
An appraiser is not required to include a statement that "there have been no additional sales," though a client may make such a requirement as an assignment condition.	FAQ 261, page 298
What to disclose when there have been no sales in the last three years	
There is no requirement stating "there have been no sales" in the three-year period.	FAQ 261, page 298
The requirement is only to analyze any prior sales and to report on those prior sales.	FAQ 261, page 298; Standards Rule 1-5(b), page 19, lines 560-561; Standards Rule 2-2(a)(x)(3), page 21, lines 625-626
Of the subject property when the subject property is used as a comparable	
If a prior sale of a subject property occurred within three years, that sale must be analyzed.	FAQ 249, page 294; Standards Rule 1-5(b), page 19, lines 560-561
Of the comparable sales	
USPAP does not have a specific requirement to analyze prior sales of comparable properties; however, there may be assignment conditions that require this.	FAQ 253, page 296
How far back in time to analyze prior sales (real property)	
An assignment condition may include the need to analyze prior sales of the subject property more than three years prior to the effective date. Since this exceeds the minimum USPAP requirement for real property appraisals, this is allowed.	FAQ 250, page 294; COMPETENCY RULE, page 11, line 309
How far back in time to analyze prior sales (personal property)	
USPAP does not prescribe a time period. The appraiser is only required to, if relevant, analyze all prior sales that occurred within a reasonable and applicable time period.	FAQ 263, page 299; Standard 7-5(b), page 45, lines 1445-1446
Prior sales of a portion of the subject property	
The appraiser is required to analyze all prior sales of a subject property, even if a prior sale was only a sale of a portion of the subject property.	FAQ 251, page 295; Standards Rule 1-5(b), page 19, lines 560-561
Prior sales history for a retrospective appraisal	
Analysis is required for listing that was "current as of the effective date" of the appraisal, not as of the date of the report.	FAQ 259, page 298; Standards Rule 1-5(a), page 19, lines 558-559; Standards Rule 2-2(a)(x)(3), page 21, lines 625-626

SECTION ONE GUIDE TO USPAP-RELATED TOPICS

Analyze "Restrictions" or Encumbrances

What are these?

They are something that prohibits a property owner from exercising any of the traditional rights of ownership.	FAQ 221, page 280
They may impact value.	FAQ 221, page 280

Examples

Constraints on the exhibition of a work of art, a prohibition or limit on the breeding of an animal, the limit on the sale of an item.	FAQ 221, page 280

How to handle

They may or may not impact value; however, the appraiser is required to analyze the effect on value, if any.	FAQ 222, page 280; Standards Rule 7-4(d), page 44, lines 1419-1420

Analyze Supply and Demand

Sudden market conditions changes

The appraiser is required to identify, analyze, and report economic property characteristics, regardless of if they are negative or positive.	FAQ 220, page 279; Standards Rule 1-2(e), 1-3(a)(iii); 2-2(a)(iv), pages 17-18

Comparable Sales

Using the subject property as a comparable

A prior sale of a subject property could be used as a comparable.	FAQ 249, page 294; Standards Rule 1-4(a), page 18, lines 518-521

Using pending sales as comparables

Pending sales are not required to be used as comparables. However, if the lack of not considering the pending sale would constitute an omission that would impact the appraisal, then the analysis of the pending sale would be required.	FAQ 248, page 294; Standards Rule 1-1(b), page 16, line 450

Minimum number of comparable sales

USPAP does not require a minimum number of comparable sales; however, assignment conditions may require a minimum number.	FAQ 249, page 294

Data Necessary for Credible Assignment Results

Who determines what data is necessary?

The appraiser determines what data is necessary.	FAQ 144, page 249
Analyze data that has impacts on value.	FAQ 179, page 263

Exposure Time

What is it?

It is the time period the property would have been offered for sale prior to the hypothetical consummation of a sale.	FAQ 182, page 264; DEFINITION of exposure time, page 4, lines 108-110
It relates to length of time it would have taken the subject property to sell (and not the neighborhood as a whole).	FAQ 183, page 264
It is dependent on the characteristics of the subject property and the market conditions as of the effective date.	FAQ 183, page 264
It is a function of price, time, and use, and not an isolated opinion of time alone.	AO-35, pages 158-160

SECTION ONE GUIDE TO USPAP-RELATED TOPICS

When it is a component of the definition of value
It must be developed, unless precluded by law.

FAQ 122, page 239; FAQ 123, page 239

When is it required?
An opinion of reasonable exposure time is required whenever it is a component of the definition of value.

FAQ 182, page 264; FAQ 183, page 264; Standards Rules 1-2(c)(iv), page 43, lines 1345-1347 and 7-2(c)(iv), page 17, lines 469-471

Reported in conjunction with a range of values
It is not required that the opinion of the exposure time be linked to a range of values, rather, it just needs to be linked to an opinion of value (which may be a specific value or a range of values).

FAQ 184, page 265

Highest and Best Use

Example
Appraising two lots as if they existed as one legal lot, the appraiser may have to develop an opinion of highest and best use.

FAQ 223, page 280

Marketing Time

What is it?
It is the time period the property will likely take to sell immediately following the effective date of value.

FAQ 182, page 264

It relates to the length of time the properties in the neighborhood would sell, not to the subject property.

FAQ 183, page 264

When is it required?
USPAP does not require it be developed, but a client might.

FAQ 182, page 264

Tools, Methods, Techniques, and Approaches to Value

Reconciliation of approaches to value
Is required.

FAQ 210, page 276; Standards Rule 1-6, page 19, lines 563-566

Which ones are prescribed?
USPAP does not prescribe methods or techniques for any assignment.

FAQ 194, page 268

The appraiser must be aware of, understand, and correctly employ the recognized methods and techniques that are necessary for credible assignment results.

FAQ 194, page 268; Standards Rule 1-1(a), page 16, lines 436-438

Does USPAP offer guidance on methods?
No. USPAP focuses on standards, not methods.

FAQ 204, page 272

USPAP does not place limitations on the size of adjustments that may be made when using the sales comparison approach.

FAQ 211, page 276

USPAP only states the appraiser must be aware of, understand, and correctly employ the correct methods.

FAQ 204, page 272; COMPETENCY RULE, page 11, lines 305-315

USPAP requires an appraiser be competent.

FAQ 204, page 272

Discounted Cash Flow Analysis is discussed in AO-33.

FAQ 326, page 32

SECTION ONE GUIDE TO USPAP-RELATED TOPICS

Sales comparison approach

USPAP does not have any limits on the size of adjustments for comparable sales, though some clients may address this issue.
FAQ 211, page 276

Income approach

An appraiser is required to analyze specific data related to an income approach if the client expects it or if an appraiser's peers would do as much.
FAQ 228, page 283; SCOPE OF WORK RULE, Acceptability, page 14, lines 385-387

Cost approach

Only needs to be completed when it is necessary for credible assignment results.
FAQ 194, page 268; Standards Rule 1-4(b), page 18, lines 522-527

It is up to the appraiser to know when it is to be completed.
FAQ 194, page 268

The decision to use the cost approach is part of the scope of work decision.
FAQ 205, page 272

Examples of tools

An appraiser can use an Automated Valuation Model (AVM) as a tool.
FAQ 199, page 270

When an appraiser uses an AVM generated report as a tool, the appraisal report should be clear how the appraiser is using the tool (either as data that informs an appraisal assignment, or as output that the client wants the appraiser to run).
FAQ 200, page 270

Examples of method

Mass appraisal is a method. It is not a discipline.
FAQ 202, page 271; STANDARD 5

Blockage discount is a method.
FAQ 203, page 272; FAQ 204, page 272; STANDARD 5

Opinion of Value

What is it?

For example, an opinion of market rent is an opinion of value (as it is an expression of value for the right to use a property).
FAQ 177, page 263

A range of values is an opinion of value.
FAQ 186, page 266; DEFINITION of appraisal, page 3, lines 64-66

An opinion of value is an appraisal.
FAQ 186, page 266

Intentionally inflating or deflating

It is a violation of the ETHICS RULE to intentionally deflate an opinion of value.
FAQ 180, page 263; ETHICS RULE, Conduct, Page 7, lines 184-207

Matching a contract price

An appraiser's job is not to conclude an opinion of value that matches a contract price, rather it is to remain impartial, objective, and independent while forming an opinion of value.
FAQ 257, page 297; ETHICS RULE, Conduct, page 7, lines 185-186

The appraiser is required to analyze any agreements of sale (that are available during the normal course of business), which is different than how an opinion of value is reached. The information informs the appraiser but does not drive the value conclusion.
FAQ 257, page 297; Standards Rule 2-2(a)(x)(3), page 21, lines 625-626; ETHICS RULE, Conduct, page 7, lines 185-186

SECTION ONE GUIDE TO USPAP-RELATED TOPICS

Physical Characteristics

What they are
They are attributes of a property that are observable as fact.

FAQ 75, page 218; Definitions, page 5, lines 151-152

Examples include a property address, year of construction, number of bedrooms.

FAQ 76, page 218; FAQ 77, page 219; FAQ 78, page 219; FAQ 79, page 220; FAQ 80, page 220

What they are not
Something that is the appraiser's opinion or conclusion such as identifying "functional problems" or a "dated décor."

FAQ 76, page 218

Are they confidential?
No.

FAQ 75, page 218

Personal Inspection

What is a personal inspection?
It is not, for example, inspecting only photos of a property.

FAQ 191, page 267

When does it occur in the process?
If one is done, it can be done at any point in the process.

FAQ 229, page 283

Can I use a drone to inspect a property?
Yes, but it is not a personal inspection.

FAQ 226, page 281; DEFINITION of personal inspection, page 5, lines 140-145

Can someone else perform a property inspection?
Yes. An appraiser can use the information provided to them about the property; however, there are other considerations to keep in mind.

FAQ 227, page 282

Reasonable Steps

What they are
Sound judgment, reasonable steps, and practical solutions in context of the issue.

FAQ 81, page 221

Where they are referenced
In relation to safeguarding access to confidential information.

FAQ 81, page 221; ETHICS RULE, Confidentiality, page 9, lines 255-256

Relevant Data

Who determines what is relevant data?
The appraiser determines what data is relevant.

FAQ 144, page 248

Significant Appraisal Assistance

What is it?

The contribution is of substance to the development of assignment results and the contribution is related to the appraisal process or requires appraiser competency.	**FAQ 278, page 304**
If the assistance includes deciding what, where, or how to research, then the appraiser has applied judgment, and applying judgment or performing analysis for an assignment would likely be considered significant appraisal assistance.	**FAQ 280, page 306**
If the service provided includes performing tasks that require appraisal competency, for example, rating a property's quality or condition, estimating remaining economic life, and selecting comparable data.	**FAQ 279, page 305**
For example, it has likely occurred when an appraiser has determined value is impacted or influenced by the one who provided the significant appraisal assistance.	**FAQ 288, page 311**

What is it not?

For example, when an appraiser of a different discipline provides a result to another appraiser, and this receiving appraiser relies on the result, then uses an extraordinary assumption when referring to that first appraiser's conclusions.	**FAQ 284, page 307**
For example, when four personal property appraisers, with different specialties, work on one assignment.	**FAQ 292, page 312; Standards Rule 8-3(b), page 50, line 1624**

Trainee rights to workfile

The trainee appraiser, who provided significant appraisal assistance must, like any appraiser, maintain access to workfiles.	**FAQ 89, page 225**

How to give it recognition in an oral report

To the extent that is possible, address the significant assistance in the oral report.	**FAQ 281, page 306; Standards Rule 2-4, page 24, lines 741-742**

SECTION ONE GUIDE TO USPAP-RELATED TOPICS

TOPICS RELATED TO APPRAISAL REPORTING

ASSIGNMENT RESULTS

"Preliminary Results"

Are not defined
USPAP does not define, for example, a "preliminary estimate of value," but it does define what an appraisal is.

FAQ 117, page 236

Without a Resulting Report

The workfile
A workfile still needs to exist, if assignment results were communicated but a report was not issued.

FAQ 104, page 230; RECORD KEEPING RULE, page 10, line 265

Sharing (or Reusing) Information

Reusing information from a prior appraisal report
An appraiser might be able to use information and analysis from a prior assignment for a new assignment; however, be aware of confidential information and the requirements around it.

FAQ 215, page 277; ETHICS RULE, Confidentiality, page 9, lines 248-254

Communicating Assignment Results

Before completion of the assignment
Is allowed.

FAQ 104, page 230; FAQ 299, page 316; FAQ 329, page 327

Before issuance of a report
USPAP allows the appraiser to communicate results to a client prior to the issuance of a report.

FAQ 110, page 231; FAQ 333, page 329

However, if a value opinion is communicated, then the appraiser must comply with the USPAP reporting requirements.

FAQ 325, page 325

Credible Assignment Results

Data used to reach results
The appraiser determines what data is relevant and necessary for credible assignment results.

FAQ 144, page 249

How to measure
Credible assignment results are measured in the context of the intended use of the assignment.

FAQ 170, page 260

They will depend on the assignment.

FAQ 193, page 268

SECTION ONE GUIDE TO USPAP-RELATED TOPICS

Relative, not absolute
Credibility is relative, not absolute, because it is measured in the context of the intended use of the assignment.
FAQ 170, page 260

Require support
Credible assignment results require support, by relevant evidence and logic, to the degree necessary for the intended use.
DEFINITION of Credible, page 4, lines 104-105

Depend on the intended use
Assignment results that are credible for one intended use may not be credible for another intended use.
FAQ 170, page 260

THE REPORT: HOW TO REPORT

Reporting and Errors

Errors of commission
An error of commission is doing something incorrectly.
FAQ 171, page 261; Standards Rule 1-1(b), page 16, line 450

An example is incorrectly identifying the subject property's relevant characteristics such as inaccurately measuring a home.
FAQ 171, page 261; FAQ 190, page 267

Errors of omission
An error of omission is neglecting to do something that is necessary.
FAQ 171, page 261; Standards Rule 1-1(b), page 16, line 450

An example is failing to identify a subject property's relevant characteristic.
FAQ 171, page 261; FAQ 190, page 267

Making a series of errors
The appraiser should not render appraisal services in a careless or negligent manner, such as making a series of errors.
FAQ 172, page 261; Standards Rules 1-1(c), 7-1(c), 9-1(c)

Reporting and "Misleading"

Examples of "misleading"
Changing the name of the client on the report.
FAQ 133, page 244

Communicating a report or assignment results in a way that is known by the appraiser to be misleading.
ETHICS RULE, page 7, lines 194-195

Knowingly permitting someone else to communicate a report or assignment results in a way that is misleading.
ETHICS RULE, page 7, lines 196-197

Advertising in a way that misleading.
ETHICS RULE, page 8, lines 235

An appraiser's lack of knowledge and understanding could lead to misleading conclusions.
AO-14, page 83, lines 39-40

Failure to extract pertinent market information can produce conclusions that are misleading.
AO-16, page 86, lines 71-74

Failure to include sufficient information.
AO-3, page 73, line 50

Failure to include information that is specific to the assignment.
AO-3, page 73, lines 59-67

Removing data from a report that the appraiser considered relevant.
FAQ 142, page 247

Reporting stable values when the appraiser knows the market is declining.
FAQ 185, page 265

Certifying that a personal inspection was done when all that was done was to look at photos of the property.
FAQ 191, page 267

Appraising only a physical segment of a property and not communicating in the report the existence of the parts not included in the value.	FAQ 195, page 268
Not appropriately disclosing information about the unavailability of a sales contract.	FAQ 208, page 275 |◊
Requirements to not be misleading	
Do not change the name of the client on the report.	FAQ 133, page 244
Do not knowingly communicate a report or assignment results in a way that is misleading.	**ETHICS RULE, page 7, lines 194-195**
Do not knowingly permit someone else to communicate a report or assignment results in a way that is misleading.	**ETHICS RULE, page 7, lines 196-197**
Do not advertise in a way that is false, misleading, or exaggerated.	**ETHICS RULE, page 8, lines 235**
Do not communicate any analysis, opinion, or conclusion in a manner that is misleading.	**STANDARD 2, page 20, lines 567-568; STANDARD 4, page 29, lines 866-867; STANDARD 6, page 38, lines 1179-1180; STANDARD 8, page 46, lines 1453-1454; STANDARD 10, page 54, lines 1741-1743**
Write the appraisal clearly and accurately.	**STANDARD 2, page 20, line 575; STANDARD 4, page 29, line 874; STANDARD 6, page 38, line 1187; STANDARD 8, page 46, line 1461; STANDARD 10, page 54, line 1751**
Misleading vs. competency	
An appraiser who, for example, indicates a market is stable when they know it is declining, is being misleading. If the appraiser did not know how to properly recognize a market is declining, may also be in violation of other requirements in the development standard and in the COMPETENCY RULE.	FAQ 185, page 265

THE REPORT: CONTENT

Applicability

When are reporting requirements applicable?	
Whenever a value opinion is communicated.	FAQ 325, page 325
For example: selecting and providing a client with comps for a known subject property.	FAQ 325, page 325
For example: telling a property owner their tax assessment is too high.	FAQ 325, page 325
For example: providing an opinion of market rent.	FAQ 325, page 325
For example: analyzing and communicating the results of an AVM for a property in an appraisal assignment.	FAQ 325, page 325

Approaches to Value

Performing an unnecessary approach	
Is allowed, so long as the appraiser properly addresses the applicability and suitability of the approach.	FAQ 330, page 328

Client

Identify the client
In the report, unless the client has requested anonymity, the name of the client must be stated.

FAQ 316, page 322; Standards Rules 2-2(a)(i) and (b), 6-2(a), 8-2(a) and (b) and 10-2(a)

Why identify the client
It allows the client to recognize their relationship to the assignment and the report.

FAQ 317, page 322

Confidential Information

Pending sales comparable details
These details are often confidential, and the appraiser must not disclose information they know is confidential (when the information is classified as confidential by law or regulation).

FAQ 248, page 294, Definition of Confidential Information, page 4, line 101; Standards Rule 1-1(b), page 16, line 450

Copy of an Appraiser's License, Resume, etc.

Not specifically required by USPAP
There are no requirements in USPAP specifying that an appraiser's credentials be identified in an appraisal report; however, it may be an assignment condition to do so.

FAQ 303, page 318; FAQ 304, page 318; FAQ 328, page 327

Data Input

Who can input data into the report?
A data entry company can input data into a report; however, there are concerns about this the appraiser should be aware of.

FAQ 279, page 305

Dates

Appraisal date
USPAP does not define this or use this term.

FAQ 148, page 251

Date of report
Is not defined in USPAP, but is referenced in the reporting standards.

Standards Rule 2-2(a)(vii), page 21, line 615

It is the date when the report is completed and transmitted to the client and not the date the report was started.

FAQ 151, page 252

"Current" date
A current date means it is contemporaneous with the date of the report.

FAQ 155, page 254; AO-34, page 156, lines 15-17

Date of "revised" report
The date of the revised report should be the date it is completed and transmitted to the client.

FAQ 152, page 252

Date of certification
If there is a certification date, it should only be based on the date a report is completed and transmitted, because an appraiser cannot certify what they have done until they have done it.

FAQ 151, page 252

SECTION ONE GUIDE TO USPAP-RELATED TOPICS

A signed and dated certification is required for all oral reports.	RECORD KEEPING RULE, page 10, lines 274-275

Date of appraisal

This is an ambiguous term and is not defined in USPAP.	FAQ 148, page 251

Effective date

Is defined in USPAP.	Definition of effective date, page 4, lines 106-107
The date of the opinion of value.	FAQ 143, page 248
It establishes the context for the value opinion.	FAQ 143, page 248
USPAP does not dictate a format for stating the effective date.	FAQ 147, page 251; Standards Rule 2-2(a)(vii)
The effective date does not have to be cited next to every value opinion.	FAQ 149, page 251
The effective date can be changed, but additional steps must be taken (depending on where the assignment is in the process).	FAQ 150, page 251; SCOPE OF WORK RULE, Problem Identification, page 13, line 369
The appraiser does not have to have competency as of the effective date of the appraisal, rather, they have to have competency as of the time they are developing a value opinion.	FAQ 156, page 254; COMPETENCY RULE, page 11, lines 298-300

Expiration date

An appraisal report does not have an expiration date.	FAQ 143, page 248

Multiple effective dates

One assignment can require two opinions of value and one report can contain two value opinions.	FAQ 157, page 254; FAQ 159, page 255

Post-value information

An appraiser cannot include in the analysis an event that happened subsequent to the effective date.	FAQ 158, page 255

Prospective date

While not defined in USPAP, valuing a property based on a prospective date is allowed.	FAQ 154, page 253

Report date

It means the same thing as "date of report."	FAQ 148, page 251
Report date is not defined in USPAP, or used in USPAP, though it does appear in some guidance.	FAQ 153, page 253; FAQ 151, page 252; FAQ 148, page 251
It indicates the perspective of the appraiser (as current, retrospective, or prospective).	FAQ 143, page 248

Retrospective date

The appraiser does not have to have competency as of the retrospective date of the appraisal, rather, they have to have competency as of the time they are developing a value opinion.	FAQ 156, page 254; COMPETENCY RULE, page 11, lines 298-300
Be aware of how to handle information which occurred after the effective date (that cannot be included in the analysis).	FAQ 158, page 255
The appraiser would comply with the edition of USPAP effective as of the date of the report (not as of the effective date of the value opinion).	FAQ 160, page 256
Using comparable sales after the effective date in a retrospective appraisal might be misleading.	FAQ 161, page 256

SECTION ONE GUIDE TO USPAP-RELATED TOPICS

Signature date
This is sometimes used by an appraiser to indicate when a report was transmitted to a client, but it is a term that is not used, or defined in USPAP.

FAQ 148, page 251

Start date of report
USPAP has no requirements to state when a report was started.

FAQ 151, page 252

Information That May or May Not Be Necessary in the Report

Legal description
USPAP does not specifically require an appraisal report include a legal description; however, that information may be needed to convey the property characteristics relevant to the assignment.

FAQ 309, page 319; Standards Rule 2-2(a), page 21, lines 602-603; Standards Rule 8-2(a)(iv) and Standards Rule 10-2(a)(iv)

Property address
USPAP does not specifically require an appraisal report include a property address, the requirement, rather, is that the appraiser provide sufficient information to identify the real estate involved in the appraisal.

FAQ 310, page 320; Standards Rule 2-2(a), page 21, lines 601-603

Intended Use

Identify the intended use
The disclosure of the intended use is to avoid misleading parties in possession of an appraisal.

FAQ 318, page 323

For clarity, one might state that other intended uses are not intended.

FAQ 318, page 323

Multiple intended uses in one report
A report may be for more than one intended use.

FAQ 319, page 323

Intended Users

Identify the intended users
In the report, identify the intended users by name or type (depending on what type of reporting option is used).

FAQ 315, page 322; AO-36, page 161-164

If the report is a Restricted Appraisal Report, other intended users must be identified by name.

FAQ 334, page 329

Photos

Altering photos
An appraiser can alter photos so long as the action does not result in a misleading report.

FAQ 331, page 328

Reporting the Exclusion of Approaches

How to report the exclusion of an approach
Provide some basis for the opinion as to why the approach was not necessary, so that the intended users have insight into why the analysis was not performed.

FAQ 313, page 321

SECTION ONE GUIDE TO USPAP-RELATED TOPICS

Reporting the Scope of Work

Why report it?
It gives the intended users a clear understanding of the extent of the research and analysis performed.

FAQ 311, page 320; SCOPE OF WORK RULE, page 14, lines 406-407

The importance of proper disclosure of the scope of work
Proper disclosure of the scope of work is required because clients and other intended users rely on assignment results.

FAQ 311, page 320

It communicates the scope of work actually performed, not the scope of work planned.

AO-28, page 137, lines 83-86

Where to include it in the report
USPAP does not say where it should be disclosed, thus, the scope of work disclosure can be throughout the report, or in one or more sections.

FAQ 314, page 321; SCOPE OF WORK RULE, Disclosure obligations, page 14, lines 403 to 412

Source and Definition of Value

Fannie Mae 1004 form
The form does contain the source and definition of value on it.

FAQ 162, page 257

Information That Was Analyzed

Appraisal Report
The report must contain a summary of information that was analyzed.

FAQ 142, page 248; Standards Rule 2-2(a)(x)(5), page 21, lines 631-632

Restricted Appraisal Report
A summary of the information analyzed is not required.

Standards Rule 2-2(b)(xii)(4), page 23, lines 679-682

Negative Property Issues

Adverse issues
The appraiser is not required to report adverse conditions to other authorities, unless required by law.

FAQ 53, page 209; FAQ 54, page 209

If required by law to report the issue, it is not a jurisdictional exception.

FAQ 54, page 209

Multiple Opinions of Value

Contained in one report
Are allowed, and both (or more) opinions of value must be developed in conformance with the applicable development standard.

FAQ 157, page 254

Signature

What is it?
It is personalized evidence accepting the content in the report.

FAQ 272, page 302; DEFINITION of Signature, page 5, lines 164-165

SECTION ONE GUIDE TO USPAP-RELATED TOPICS

An appraiser signing the report, accepts responsibility for the assignment results related to their appraisal discipline.	FAQ 275, page 304; Standards Rule 2-3(b), page 24, lines 720-721

Who can sign

A business entity can sign an appraisal report, but only an individual appraiser can sign a certification.	FAQ 277, page 304; Standards Rule 2-3(b), page 24, line 720

Who should not sign

An appraiser who provided significant appraisal assistance and who disagrees with the supervisor's opinions and conclusions stated in the report.	FAQ 285, page 309; Standards Rule 2-3(b), page 24, lines 720-728

Can the signature be stored in a digital file?

Yes, it can be stored in a digital file to be used with the appraiser's authorization.	FAQ 273, page 303

Authorizing use of a signature

An appraiser may authorize the use of his or her signature.	FAQ 272, page 302 ETHICS RULE, Management, page 8, line 238
The authorization may only be given on a case-by-case basis.	FAQ 272, page 302; ETHICS RULE, Management, page 8, line 238

Unauthorized use of a signature

An appraiser is not liable for unauthorized use of their signature.	FAQ 274, page 303; ETHICS RULE, Management, page 8, lines 240-241

Required in the certification

USPAP requires a signed certification, not a signed report.	FAQ 269, page 302
If the report is electronic, the report must contain a signed certification.	FAQ 276, page 304

If an appraiser signs a report, also sign the certification

If an appraiser signs a report, they must sign the certification.	FAQ 269, page 302; Standards Rule 2-3(a), page 24, lines 720-721

If an appraiser signs a letter of transmittal in a report, also sign the certification

USPAP only requires the appraiser to sign the certification; however, if they sign a letter of transmittal, they must sign the certification.	FAQ 270, page 302; Standards Rule 2-3(b), page 24, lines 720-721

If two appraisers sign a report, they must also sign the certification

If an appraiser (or if multiple appraisers) signs any part of a report, then the appraiser must also sign the certification.	FAQ 271, page 302; Standards Rule 2-3(b), page 24, lines 720-721

Significant Appraisal Assistance

Where to disclose

Must be disclosed somewhere (anywhere) in the report.	FAQ 283, page 307

Disclose that person's name in the certification

The name of the person providing the significant appraisal assistance must be included in the certification.	FAQ 297, page 315

SECTION ONE GUIDE TO USPAP-RELATED TOPICS

Information for Others Who Read the Report

They will not be misled since they are not identified as users or clients.
Parties other than clients or intended users, when reading the report, will see they are not identified as a user and this "puts them on notice."

FAQ 317, page 322

Work Not Done

Is there a need to report work not done in an assignment?
Sometimes there is, if it helps the intended users understand the scope of work.

FAQ 312, page 321; SCOPE OF WORK RULE, Disclosure Obligations, page 14, lines 407-408

THE REPORT: DRAFT

Draft Reports

Are sometimes appropriate
Draft reports are not defined in USPAP, though they are a part of some types of appraisal practice.

FAQ 329, page 327

THE REPORT: FORMS

Forms (in general)

Forms that comply with USPAP
Appraisers comply with USPAP, not forms.

FAQ 167, page 258; FAQ 324, page 325

Alternate Valuation Products

Do they comply with USPAP?
An appraiser complies with USPAP, not forms.

FAQ 167, page 258

So long as the use of the form results in the appraiser being able to comply with USPAP, any type of form is acceptable.

FAQ 167, page 258

Condition and Marketability Reports

Reports about condition, even though they do not include a value opinion, are covered by USPAP.
A condition report pertains to value, thus, filling out this form is a valuation service, and you are being asked to fill out the form as an appraiser.

FAQ 29, page 199; DEFINITION of valuation service, page 5, lines 166-167; DEFINITION of appraisal practice, page 3, lines 67-68

Drive-by or Desktop Appraisals

An inspection is not required by USPAP.
This type of form is just an appraisal without an interior inspection done as part of the scope of work.

FAQ 189, page 266

SECTION ONE GUIDE TO USPAP-RELATED TOPICS

Fannie Mae Form 1004

Labeling the report
If a report has the term "Summary Appraisal Report" written on it, then this can mean it is labeled correctly.

FAQ 301, page 317

Source and Definition of Value
The form does contain the source and definition of value.

FAQ 162, page 257

"Stable" and "Declining" boxes
Check what box is correct, not one that the underwriter would like to see checked.

FAQ 185, page 265

Certification statements
If a form that an appraiser is required to use in the reporting of the appraisal does not have the correct certification statements, it is still the responsibility of the appraiser to comply with USPAP.

FAQ 24, page 197; Standards Rule 2-3(a), page 23, lines 701-703

If an appraiser has certified they have personally inspected the property, then that must be true (and just inspecting photos of the property is not a personal inspection).

FAQ 191, page 267

If an appraiser has certified they have personally inspected the exterior of the comparable sales, they must have done so.

FAQ 192, page 268

If an appraiser is required to certify they have personally inspected the exterior of the comparable sales, but are not required to (and do not need to, for the sake of credible assignment results) inspect the exterior of active listings.

FAQ 193, page 268

Fannie Mae allows the appraiser to add additional certification statements to their form, or may add a supplemental certification to the report.

FAQ 294, page 314; FAQ 295, page 314; FAQ 268, page 301; Standards Rule 2-3(a) page 23, lines 690- 719

Fannie Mae Form 1004D

"The property has not decreased in value"
This is an appraisal and thus, the appraiser must comply with the development and reporting requirements of an appraisal.

FAQ 213, page 277; Definition of appraisal, page 3, lines 62-66

Making this statement is a new appraisal.

FAQ 308, page 319; AO-3, pages 72-73

How much information to include in the report for an "update"
The appraiser will need to supplement the form as necessary, so that the resulting appraisal report complies with Standards Rule 2-2 (a).

FAQ 308, page 319)

Does updating an appraisal require a certification?
Yes. An appraisal update is a new assignment because an appraisal update is an appraisal.

FAQ 289, page 311

Does a final inspection require a certification?
No. A final inspection is not an appraisal.

FAQ 290, page 312

Can a prior certification be incorporated by reference?
No. One cannot certify past work for work that will be done in the future.

FAQ 289, page 311

No need to REPORT a prior service in a certification if a value is not provided on this form.
So long as the 1004D is the form that is used, and this is not an appraisal or an appraisal review assignment, then a certification is not required.

FAQ 266, page 301; ETHICS RULE, page 8, line 218-219

46 USPAP Reference Manual © 2022 The Appraisal Foundation

SECTION ONE GUIDE TO USPAP-RELATED TOPICS

Need to DISCLOSE a prior service
Even if the 1004D form is not a part of an appraisal or appraisal review assignment (and thus, a certification statement is not required to be added to the form), the appraiser must still disclose to the client (either at the time of the assignment or upon discovery) if a prior service was performed.

FAQ 266, page 301; ETHICS RULE, page 8, line 218-219

Fannie Mae Form 1004MC

Does the certification apply to this addendum?
Yes, since it is identified as part of the report, the certification does cover this form when it is included in the report.

FAQ 286, page 309

Transmittal Letter (Letter of Transmittal)

It is not required by USPAP to have one in a report
However, if one is added, there are requirements that apply.

FAQ 302, page 317

If one is included in a report, then the following requirements apply:
Any applicable disclosure about fees paid (or a thing of value given) in connection with the procurement of an assignment.

FAQ 35, page 202; ETHICS RULE, Management, page 8, lines 221-226

An appraiser who signs a letter of transmittal, must also sign a certification.

Standards Rule 2-3(b), page 24, lines 720-721; Standards Rule 6-3(b), page 40, lines 1285-1286; Standards Rule 8-3(b), page 50, lines 1616-1617; Standards Rule 10-3(b), page 57, lines 1873-1874

A reviewer who signs a letter of transmittal, must also sign a certification.

Standards Rule 4-3(b), page 31, lines 961-962

If one is included in a report, the following are not requirements:
The amount of a fee paid in the procurement of an assignment is not required to be disclosed.

FAQ 46, page 206

THE REPORT: RESTRICTED APPRAISAL REPORT

Restricted Appraisal Report

When is it <u>in</u>appropriate?
For example, when users are known and identified by type, because then an abbreviated report may not contain enough information.

FAQ 139, page 247; Standards Rule 2-2(b), page 22, lines 649-650

When is it allowed?
Can be used if there is an intended user other than the client.

FAQ 305, page 318; Standards Rule 2-2(b)(ii), page 22, line 648

Required Content
The required content is a minimum, and the appraiser can exceed this minimum.

FAQ 327, page 327

Unless the report meets the minimum content requirement for an Appraisal Report, it must still be labeled a Restricted Appraisal Report.

FAQ 327, page 327

For multiple parties
Intended users other than just the client are allowed.

FAQ 334, page 329

SECTION ONE GUIDE TO USPAP-RELATED TOPICS

THE REPORT: THE DIGITAL OR HARDCOPY

How to Label the Report

Additional labels

An appraiser can use a label in addition to "Appraisal Report" or "Restricted Appraisal Report," but they cannot use a label in place of one of these two labels.

FAQ 300, page 317; Standards Rule 2-2, page 20, lines 583-584; Standards Rule 8-2, page 46, lines 1469-1470; and Standards Rule 10-2, page 54, lines 1760-1761

Mass appraisal is different

Mass appraisal does not require a label on the report.

Standards Rule 6-2, page 38

Who Owns the Report?

Not specified

USPAP does not specifically address this; however, USPAP does address the appraiser's obligation to protect the confidential information in that report.

FAQ 298, page 316; ETHICS RULE, Confidentiality, page 8, lines 243, and page 9, lines 248-254

Sample Reports

How to provide them

If providing them, without client authorization, be sure to redact confidential information.

FAQ 59, page 211

Make certain to comply with the Confidentiality section of the ETHICS RULE.

FAQ 59, page 211; ETHICS RULE, Confidentiality, page 8, lines 242-264

How not to provide them

Do not send the redacted information to the potential client in a separate email in conjunction with a copy of the report that has been redacted.

FAQ 60, page 212

Who the appraiser may provide a copy to

Only someone that the client authorizes: not someone the appraiser chooses.

FAQ 61, page 212; ETHICS RULE, Confidentiality, page 9, line 250

Security of the Reports

Email, is it secure?

Sending a report to a client via email does not violate confidentiality requirements.

FAQ 62, page 213

Copy of the Written Report

Who the appraiser may provide a copy to

Someone that the client authorizes: not someone the appraiser chooses.

FAQ 61, page 212; ETHICS RULE, Confidentiality, page 9, line 250

Those parties authorized by law to receive a copy.

FAQ 66, page 214; ETHICS RULE, Confidentiality, page 9, line 251

A sworn peace officer who is qualified as having the authority by law to do so.

(FAQ 67, page 214; ETHICS RULE, Confidentiality, page 9, line 252

Peer review committees.

FAQ 68, page 215; ETHICS RULE, Confidentiality, page 9, line 253

"True Copy"

What is a "true copy"?

A photocopy or an electronic copy of the entire appraisal report transmitted to the client is a true copy.

FAQ 84, page 223; FAQ 100, page 228; RECORD KEEPING RULE, page 10, lines 272-273

A replica of what was sent to the client is a true copy.

FAQ 93, page 227

Contents of a true copy

Any signatures that were affixed to a report must exist on the true copy.

FAQ 93, page 227

Is it possible to keep a true copy of an oral report?

No. The requirement to keep a true copy only applies to the written report.

RECORD KEEPING RULE, page 10, line 271

Paper Copies

A paper copy is not required to be retained

Rather, only a "true copy" of the written report is required to be retained, and thus, that one copy can be digital.

FAQ 323, page 325

Delivery

Email or electronic delivery

Sending a report to a client via email is an acceptable method of communicating the appraisal report.

FAQ 62, page 213

Communication of assignment results must be done in a way that is not misleading, or that is the transmission of a fraudulent report.

FAQ 299, page 316; ETHICS RULE, Conduct, page 7, lines 193-194

The appraiser must know what exactly is being transmitted to the client; however, after the appraiser has transmitted the report, the appraiser cannot control what a client or intended user does with the report.

FAQ 299, page 316

Text messages can be appraisal reports

Text messages are written communications, and they can be the communication of assignment results and thus, they are subject to Standards Rule 2-2 (for real property).

FAQ 306, page 318

Plagiarism

It is unethical

The appraiser cannot present an appraisal report and represent it as their work; that would be misleading.

FAQ 12, page 192; ETHICS RULE, Conduct, lines, page 7, 196-197

Copyrighting

Is it allowed?

The ASB takes no position of if an appraisal report can, cannot, should, or should not be copyrighted.

FAQ 71, page 216; ETHICS RULE, Confidentiality, line 250

SECTION ONE GUIDE TO USPAP-RELATED TOPICS

Words an Appraiser Can Use

Using "high," "low," "good," etc.
USPAP does not prohibit the use of qualitative terms, though contextual information is useful.
FAQ 13, page 193

THE REPORT: THE ORAL REPORT

Workfile

Contents of workfile

The workfile must contain a summary of the oral report.
FAQ 95, page 227; FAQ 97, page 227; FAQ 320, page 324

The summary of the oral report must be added to workfile "within a reasonable time" after issuance.
RECORD KEEPING RULE, page 10, lines 267-268

The workfile must contain a signed and dated certification.
FAQ 320, page 324; RECORD KEEPING RULE, page 10, lines 274-275

Transcript of any testimony

A transcript of testimony given is not required for the workfile, so long as a summary of the testimony is in the workfile.
FAQ 95, page 227; RECORD KEEPING RULE, page 10, lines 267-268

When testimony is given, the workfile must contain either a transcript of the testimony or a summary of the testimony.
FAQ 96, page 227; RECORD KEEPING RULE, page 10, lines 274-275

When giving testimony about a written report, the signed certification must be in the true copy of the report in the workfile.
FAQ 98, page 228

The workfile, if it contains only a transcript, it need only be of the appraiser's testimony, not anyone else's testimony.
FAQ 99, page 228

If there is no testimony given, and a report was entered into evidence in conjunction with a judicial proceeding, the requirement is still only five years maximum.
FAQ 109, page 231

THE REPORT: CERTIFICATION

What Does the Certification Apply to?

The report
If signed by one appraiser, then it applies to the entire report, including any addenda.
FAQ 286, page 309), Standards Rule 2-3(b), page 24, lines 722-724

Parts of the report
It can also, if written as such, clearly indicate which discipline-specific assignment results and report content are being certified for each appraiser (when there are multiple appraisers who have competency in different assets).
FAQ 287, page 310

Who Is Required (or Not Required) to Sign?

Non-appraisers
Non-appraisers who provide assistance need not be identified in the certification.
FAQ 278 page 304

SECTION ONE GUIDE TO USPAP-RELATED TOPICS

Appraisers
Only appraisers can sign a certification.
FAQ 278, page 304

If they sign a letter of transmittal, they must also sign the certification.
FAQ 302, page 317; Standards Rule 2-3(b), page 24, lines 720-721

Assistants
Only those who provide significant appraisal assistance can sign a certification, or, if not, then they must not be identified as having provided significant appraisal assistance.
FAQ 278, page 304

"Supervisory" appraisers
Any appraiser who signs any part of an appraisal report, must sign the certification.
FAQ 282, page 307

Appraisal firms
An individual appraiser signs a certification, not an appraisal firm.
FAQ 296, page 314, FAQ 277, page 304

Why Is it Required

Evidence of ethical obligations
It is evidence that an appraiser recognizes their ethical obligations.
FAQ 265, page 301

When a Signed Certification Is Not Required

When there is no appraisal or appraisal review report.
A signed certification is a part of a report, if there is no report, there need not be a signed certification.
FAQ 266, page 301; ETHICS RULE, page 8, lines 218-219

Content Required

Present or prospective interest
Having a present or prospective interest in a property (or in the parties involved in a transaction) can prevent an appraiser from being unbiased, they must be able to certify they performed the service ethically.
FAQ 14, page 193

Payment made in the procurement of an assignment
If a payment was made in the procurement of an assignment, this must be disclosed in the certification.
FAQ 46, page 206; ETHICS RULE, Management, page 8, lines 220-226

The exact names of any appraiser who provided significant appraisal assistance.
The certification must include the name, not, for example, the job role of the person providing the significant appraisal assistance.
FAQ 297, page 315

Content Not Required

Coercion and a predetermined result
An appraiser does not have to certify they have _not_ been coerced to provide a predetermined result.
FAQ 11, page 192

Prior services if there is no appraisal or appraisal review assignment
An appraiser only needs to disclose the prior service to the client, since there is no appraisal or appraisal review report.
FAQ 266, page 301; ETHICS RULE, page 8, line 218-219

SECTION ONE GUIDE TO USPAP-RELATED TOPICS

A word for word reiteration of each statement

The wording of the certification statements in the reporting standards is not required to be stated word for word, rather the elements of each statement in the certification must be addressed.

FAQ 267, page 301; Standards Rule 2-3(a), page 23, lines 692-693

A description of any significant appraisal assistance

The information about significant appraisal assistance does not have to be in the certification, but it must be in the report. Only the name of the person who provided the significant appraisal assistance must be in the certification.

FAQ 283, page 307

Content Not Allowed

Claiming one is "USPAP Certified"

Since there is no such credential, claiming as such would be misleading. Thus, the certification should only state that the conclusions were developed, and the report was prepared in conformity with USPAP.

FAQ 43, page 205; Certification statements in Standards Rules 2-3(a), 4-3(a), 6-3(a), 8-3(a) and 10-3(a) regarding conformity with USPAP

Signature on the Certification

Reason for the signature

It is evidence that an appraiser recognizes his or her ethical obligations in USPAP.

FAQ 265, page 301

Workfile obligations

For any report, the workfile must contain a signed certification (a copy is fine).

FAQ 93, page 227; RECORD KEEPING RULE, page 10, line 271

When not to sign the certification

If an appraiser provides significant appraisal assistance and disagrees with the conclusions the supervisory appraiser reached, then the appraiser should not sign the certification (which says the opinions in the report are the appraiser's personal opinions).

FAQ 285, page 309

Multiple signatures

Are allowed, and if there is more than one signature, then each appraiser accepts responsibility for all elements in the certification.

FAQ 291, page 312

Date on Certification

This is not required.

An appraiser is required to state the date of the report, not the date of the certification.

FAQ 151, page 252; Standards Rule 2-2(a)(vii), page 21, line 615 and Standards Rule 2-2(b)(ix), page 22, line 664

If it is stated

Then it must accurately be based on the report date, since one cannot certify something as of a certain date before the thing being certified to was done.

FAQ 151, page 252

Then, if a report is revised, this date should reflect the same date as the date of the report.

FAQ 152, page 252

ISSUES THAT TYPICALLY OCCUR AFTER THE REPORT HAS BEEN DELIVERED

COMPLETION OF AN ASSIGNMENT

Modifying a Report after Completion

Could be misleading
An appraiser would be misleading if they removed a comp, at a client's request, if the appraiser concluded that comp was relevant.

FAQ 142, page 247; Standards Rule 2-2(a)(x)(5)

Changing the scope of work
The scope of work for the assignment can change after the report has been submitted, the report can then be revised and submitted.

FAQ 174, page 261

Changing the intended user
This would then be a new assignment since it was a change to an assignment element.

FAQ 174, page 262

Adding Intended Users after Completion

Is not allowed
An intended user cannot be added to the report, but an appraiser can start a new assignment.

FAQ 132, page 243

How Long Is the Report Valid for?

Expiration dates
Do not exist for appraisal reports, only users of appraisal services can determine how long they will continue to rely on the report.

FAQ 143, page 248

THE REPORT: AFTER DELIVERY TO THE CLIENT

Who Owns the Report?

USPAP does not specifically address this
USPAP, however, does address the appraiser's obligation to protect the confidential information in that report.

FAQ 298, page 316; ETHICS RULE, Confidentiality, page 8, lines 243, and page 9, lines 248-254

SECTION ONE GUIDE TO USPAP-RELATED TOPICS

Adding an Intended User

"Reliance Letters"
USPAP does not define what a reliance letter is, rather it specifies that an intended user cannot be added after the completion of an assignment (unless a new assignment is started).

FAQ 132, page 243; DEFINITION of intended user, page 4, lines 127-128

Transferring a Report (which is not allowed)

What is not allowed
A report can never be "transferred" to another party.

FAQ 133, page 244

"Release letters"
USPAP does not define a release letter, rather, it just states the client's name on a report cannot be changed.

FAQ 134, page 244

RECORD KEEPING: GENERAL CONCEPTS

When Selling an Appraisal Firm

Ethical obligations
When selling a firm, an appraiser must comply with confidentiality requirements.

FAQ 72, page 211; ETHICS RULE, Confidentiality, page 8, lines 242-247

Record keeping obligations
An appraiser must make access and retrieval arrangements to workfiles.

FAQ 72, page 217; RECORD KEEPING RULE, page 10, lines 285-287

SECTION ONE GUIDE TO USPAP-RELATED TOPICS

TOPICS RELATED TO RECORD KEEPING

RECORD KEEPING: THE WORKFILE

Creating a Workfile

When to create one

Not after the report was delivered.	**FAQ 94, page 227; RECORD KEEPING RULE, page 10, lines 265-267**
It is advisable to start a workfile as soon as the appraiser agrees to perform the assignment.	**FAQ 94, page 227**

Access to the Workfile

When access is provided to another appraiser

The person granted access has a responsibility to protect the public trust.	**FAQ 73, page 218**

When access is required

When a seller of an appraisal firm has workfile obligations.	**FAQ 73, page 217; RECORD KEEPING RULE, page 10, lines 288-293**
If a party other than the appraiser retains the workfile, that party must allow the appraiser access to the workfile under certain scenarios.	**FAQ 88, page 224; RECORD KEEPING RULE, page 10, lines 289-295**

Can access be denied?

Yes, if an appraiser is seeking access to the workfile outside of the ones specified in the RECORD KEEPING RULE.	**FAQ 91, page 226; RECORD KEEPING RULE, page 10, lines 288-295**
Because someone can deny access to the appraiser, the appraiser may wish to maintain a copy of a workfile.	**FAQ 88, page 225**
Supervisory appraiser must not impede the trainee appraiser's ability to access workfiles.	**FAQ 89, page 225**

Does an agreement for access have to be in writing?

No. USPAP does not specify how to make access arrangements.	**FAQ 92, page 226; RECORD KEEPING RULE, page 10, lines 285-286**

Format of the Workfile

Should the workfile have a specific format?

USPAP does not dictate the form or format of the workfile.	**FAQ 88, page 225**

SECTION ONE GUIDE TO USPAP-RELATED TOPICS

Contents of the Workfile

What must be in it

Items such as client information, copies of reports, and all other data to support the appraiser's opinions and conclusions.	FAQ 82, page 222; RECORD KEEPING RULE, page 10, lines 269-278
A true copy of the entire report transmitted to the client.	FAQ 84, page 223
Documents, or references in the workfile to the location of those documents.	FAQ 101, page 229; RECORD KEEPING RULE, page 10, lines 277-278

When a workfile must be prepared

For each appraisal or appraisal review assignment.	FAQ 85, page 223; DEFINITION of Assignment, page 3, line 80

Are original documents required?

No. Copies are acceptable.	FAQ 88, page 225

What must be in it for an oral report

The workfile must contain a summary of the oral report.	FAQ 95, page 227
The summary of the oral report must be added to workfile "within a reasonable time" after issuance.	RECORD KEEPING RULE, page 10, lines 267-268
A transcript of testimony given is not required for the workfile, so long as a summary of the testimony is in the workfile.	FAQ 95, page 227; RECORD KEEPING RULE, page 10, lines 267-268
When testimony is given, the workfile must contain either a transcript of the testimony or a summary of the testimony.	FAQ 96, page 227; RECORD KEEPING RULE, page 10, lines 274-275

Must be kept even if assignment is cancelled

Regardless of whether a report is issued or not, the workfile must still be retained.	FAQ 104, page 230

Existence of a Workfile

When one is required

For each appraisal or appraisal review assignment.	FAQ 104, page 230
Regardless of if the appraisal or appraisal review assignment was completed, or a report was issued, a workfile is required.	FAQ 104, page 230

Custody of a Workfile

Two appraisers: Who should have custody?

If there are two appraisers, neither appraiser is specifically required to have custody of the workfile; however, the one without custody must have arrangements for retention, access, and retrieval.	FAQ 87, page 224; RECORD KEEPING RULE, page 10, lines 285-286

If an appraiser does not have custody, what do they do?

They must make appropriate workfile retention, access, and retrieval arrangements.	FAQ 90, page 226; RECORD KEEPING RULE, page 10, lines 285-286

SECTION ONE GUIDE TO USPAP-RELATED TOPICS

Number of Workfiles

Multiple appraisers

If two appraisers sign a report, there still need only be one workfile.	FAQ 87, page 224; RECORD KEEPING RULE, page 10, lines 285-286
If there are two appraisers for one appraisal assignment, both most maintain access to the workfile.	FAQ 89, page 225

Purpose of the Workfile

What the purpose of the workfile is

To ensure performance, to facilitate enforcement, to preserve evidence of compliance with USPAP, preserve information that supports the appraiser's opinions and conclusions, and it aids the appraiser in handling questions from a client or intended user.	FAQ 82, page 222

Retention of the Workfile

Who should honor retention arrangements?

When buying an appraisal firm, an appraiser should honor any retention arrangements.	FAQ 73, page 218; RECORD KEEPING RULE, page 10, lines 288-293
The appraiser, not their employer.	FAQ 85, page 223; RECORD KEEPING RULE, page 10, lines 282-284

How long to retain a workfile?

A minimum of five years <u>and</u> a maximum of two years after final deposition of a judicial proceeding.	FAQ 109, page 231; RECORD KEEPING RULE, page 10, lines 282-284
If a state law requires only a three-year retention period, USPAP would still apply and thus, five years minimum.	FAQ 102, page 229; JURISDICTIONAL EXCEPTION RULE, page 15, lines 413-414
There is no USPAP limit on a maximum amount of time to retain the workfile.	FAQ 103, page 229

When to stop retention

An appraiser cannot destroy records any time prior to five years after preparation.	FAQ 86, page 223; RECORD KEEPING RULE, page 10, lines 265, 282-284; ETHICS RULE, Conduct page 7, line 202

Can retention stop when the appraiser is deceased?

The appraiser was responsible for retaining the workfiles, no one else.	FAQ 107, page 231
A state or other entity may require the files to be retained by someone else in this circumstance, but that is not a USPAP requirement.	FAQ 107, page 231

Who should retain the workfile?

If the appraiser does not have retention of the workfile, they must make arrangements with the party who has the workfile, to protect and preserve the file.	FAQ 88, page 224; FAQ 108, page 231
If the appraiser is an independent contractor, the appraiser is responsible for retention.	FAQ 88, page 224; RECORD KEEPING RULE, page 10, line 285
If the appraiser is an employee, the appraiser is responsible for retention.	FAQ 88, page 224; RECORD KEEPING RULE, page 10, line 285

SECTION ONE GUIDE TO USPAP-RELATED TOPICS

Because someone can deny access to the workfile to the appraiser, the appraiser may wish to maintain a copy of a workfile.
FAQ 88, page 225

Manner of workfile retention
The arrangement for workfile retention is a business arrangement.
FAQ 88, page 225

How to ensure the workfile is retained
If an appraiser does not have custody of a workfile, the appraiser can come up with any number of ways to ensure the appraiser has access to the workfile.
FAQ 90, page 226

Retrieval of the Workfile

Who should honor retrieval arrangements?
When buying an appraisal firm, an appraiser should honor any retrieval arrangements.
FAQ 73, page 218; RECORD KEEPING RULE, page 10, lines 288-293

Providing Copies of the Workfile

AMC requests a copy of the workfile
This is not prohibited; however, the appraiser must comply with confidentiality requirements.
FAQ 88, page 225

Attorney Client wants a copy of the workfile
Providing the workfile to a duly authorized party is permitted.
FAQ 88, page 225

Purging

Purging a workfile
An appraiser cannot comply with a client request to purge a workfile.
FAQ 86, page 223; RECORD KEEPING RULE, page 10, line 265, 282-284; ETHICS RULE, Conduct, page 7, line 202

Disposal or Destroying

How to dispose
USPAP does not dictate a method; however, do not violate the ETHICS RULE when disposing of files.
FAQ 83, page 222; ETHICS RULE, Confidentiality, page 9, lines 255-256

When to destroy
An appraiser cannot destroy records any time prior to five years after preparation.
FAQ 86, page 223; RECORD KEEPING RULE, page 10, line 265, 282-284; ETHICS RULE, Conduct page 7, line 202

Accidental destruction
If workfiles are accidently destroyed, there are no provisions in USPAP for this unfortunate situation.
FAQ 105, page 230; RECORD KEEPING RULE, page 10, lines 282-284

SECTION ONE GUIDE TO USPAP-RELATED TOPICS

SAME PROPERTY, NEW ASSIGNMENT[1]

Confidential Information

Don't disclose in new assignment
When appraising the same property, a second time, be careful not to disclose confidential information in the second assignment.

FAQ 15, page 194

When It May or May Not Be a New Assignment

Change of effective date
Depends where in the process the appraiser is.

FAQ 150, page 251

When It Is a New Assignment

New intended user
If an intended user wants to be "added to a report" after completion of an assignment, this cannot be done. This would need to be the start of a new assignment.

FAQ 132, page 243

New client
An appraiser cannot simply change the client's name on an old report and issue a new report; that is misleading.

FAQ 133, page 244; FAQ 168, page 259

"Update" of a prior assignment
"Update" is a new appraisal assignment that involves the same subject property as a prior assignment.

FAQ 217, page 278

"Update" is a business term. A second assignment for a client is a new assignment.

FAQ 212, page 276

Regardless of the label, an appraisal of a property that was the subject of a prior assignment is not an extension of a prior assignment, it is a new assignment.

FAQ 216, page 278

"Update" is a new assignment, and the appraiser can use any format that is acceptable for the intended use and that complies with the appropriate reporting standard.

FAQ 307, page 318; AO-3, pages 72-73

"Update" of an appraisal completed by another appraiser
This is just a new appraisal assignment.

FAQ 214, page 277; AO-3, pages 72-73

Regardless of the label, an appraisal of a property that was the subject of a prior assignment is not an extension of a prior assignment, it is a new assignment.

FAQ 216, page 278

"Update" with the appraiser indicating the property "has not decreased in value"
This is an appraisal, and it is a new assignment.

FAQ 213, page 277

Regardless of the label, an appraisal of a property that was the subject of a prior assignment is not an extension of a prior assignment, it is a new assignment.

FAQ 216, page 278

"Recertification of value"
This is not a USPAP term, but it is discussed in AO-3.

FAQ 217, page 278

If, by "recertification of value" a client means, for example, that they want a final inspection, then this is not an appraisal.

FAQ 217, page 278

Regardless of the label, an appraisal of a property that was the subject of a prior assignment is not an extension of a prior assignment, it is a new assignment.

FAQ 216, page 278

---

1 Also see "Present or Prospective Interest and Prior Services"

USPAP Reference Manual © 2022 The Appraisal Foundation   59

SECTION ONE GUIDE TO USPAP-RELATED TOPICS

"Starting Over" for a New Assignment

Does the appraiser have to start over?
No. The appraiser must decide the appropriate scope of work for the new assignment.

FAQ 215, page 277

Scope of Work for the New Assignment

New client
If the client is new, be careful to develop an appropriate scope of work consistent with the new intended use.

FAQ 132, page 244

Similar data and analysis is possible
A new assignment can include virtually the same data and analysis as a prior, similar assignment on the same subject property.

FAQ 132, page 243

Client Prohibition on Agreeing to Perform Future Assignment

Client prohibitions
The client can, upon agreeing to perform the first assignment, prohibit the appraiser from appraising the property again in the future for someone else.

FAQ 141, page 247; AO-27, page 133-135

Level of Detail in New Report

There is no minimum
An updated appraisal report is not required to have the same level of detail as the first appraisal report.

FAQ 307, page 318; AO-3, pages 72-73

APPRAISAL REVIEW

Geographic Competency

Is not required.
Geographic competency is not typically relevant, though it may be. Thus, it is assignment specific.

FAQ 336, page 330

Maintaining a Workfile

When is it required?
When there is an appraisal review assignment.

FAQ 85, page 223; DEFINITION of Assignment, page 3, line 80

Post-Valuation Date Information

Can it be used by the reviewer?
The reviewer can use the information, but not to fault the original appraiser (who would not have access to that information).

FAQ 337, page 330; Standards Rule 3-2(g), page 27, lines 818-820

"Reading" vs. "Reviewing" an Appraisal Report

Client does not ask the appraiser about the quality of the work

If the client does not ask the appraiser to assess the quality of the work of an appraisal, this is not an appraisal review.

FAQ 341, page 333

Reviewer Communicating with the Appraiser

When this is allowed

This is allowed, if the client has given their approval to the appraiser, to discuss the appraisal report with the reviewer.

FAQ 64, page 211; ETHICS RULE, Confidentiality, page 8, lines 242-264

Which Standards Apply

Standards 3 & 4

When an appraiser is developing an opinion about the quality of another's work as part of an appraisal or appraisal review assignment.

FAQ 335, page 330

These apply whenever the appraiser is, as part of an appraisal or appraisal review assignment, reviewing the work of another appraiser.

FAQ 335, page 330; Definition of Appraisal Review, page 3, lines 73-76

If a service is not an appraisal review, it must still comply with the parts of USPAP that apply to general practice.

FAQ 335, page 330

SECTION ONE GUIDE TO USPAP-RELATED TOPICS

OTHER TOPICS

THE APPRAISAL FIRM

Selling the Appraisal Firm

Ethical obligations
When selling a firm, an appraiser must comply with confidentiality requirements.

FAQ 72, page 216; ETHICS RULE, Confidentiality, page 8, lines 242-247

Record keeping obligations
An appraiser must make access and retrieval arrangements to workfiles.

FAQ 72, page 217; RECORD KEEPING RULE, page 10, lines 285-287

Buying the Appraisal Firm

Ethical obligations
When buying a firm, protect, promote, and preserve the public trust.

FAQ 73, page 217; PREAMBLE, page 1, lines 6-7; ETHICS RULE, page 13, lines 174-175)

Record keeping obligations
An appraiser must make access and retrieval arrangements to workfiles.

FAQ 72, page 217; RECORD KEEPING RULE, page 10, lines 285-287

SECTION TWO
Advisory Opinions Organized by Appraisal Discipline

SECTION TWO ADVISORY OPINIONS ORGANIZED BY APPRAISAL DISCIPLINE

Advisory Opinions Organized by Appraisal Discipline

In the USPAP publication, the AOs are organized by release date, not by topic or discipline.

In the following tables, the AOs from the 2020-2022 USPAP publication are organized by appraisal discipline: real property, personal property, and intangible property. Listed with each AO is the section of USPAP they are most applicable to.

Real Property Advisory Opinions

AO-1	Sales History
AO-2	Inspection of the Property
AO-3	Update of a Prior Appraisal
AO-7	Marketing Time Opinions
AO-9	The Appraisal of Real Property That May be Impacted by Environmental Contamination
AO-13	Performing Evaluations of Real Property Collateral to Conform with USPAP
AO-14	Appraisals for Subsidized Housing
AO-16	Fair Housing Laws and Appraisal Report Content
AO-17	Appraisals of Real Property with Proposed Improvements
AO-18	Use of an Automated Valuation Model (AVM)
AO-19	Unacceptable Assignment Conditions in Real Property Appraisal Assignments
AO-20	An Appraisal Review Assignment that Includes the Reviewer's Own Opinion of Value
AO-21	USPAP Compliance
AO-22	Scope of Work in Market Value Appraisal Assignments, Real Property
AO-23	Identifying the Relevant Characteristics of the Subject Property of a Real Property Appraisal Assignment
AO-24	Normal Course of Business
AO-25	Clarification of the Client in a Federally Related Transaction
AO-26	Readdressing (Transferring) a Report to Another Party
AO-27	Appraising the Same Property for a New Client
AO-28	Scope of Work Decision, Performance, and Disclosure
AO-29	An Acceptable Scope of Work
AO-30	Appraisals for Use by a Federally Regulated Financial Institution
AO-31	Assignments Involving More Than One Appraiser
AO-32	Ad Valorem Property Tax Appraisal and Mass Appraisal Assignments
AO-32	Discounted Cash Flow Analysis
AO-34	Retrospective and Prospective Value Opinions
AO-35	Reasonable Exposure Time in Real and Personal Property Opinions of Value
AO-36	Identification and Disclosure of Client, Intended Use, and Intended Users
AO-37	Computer Assisted Valuation Tools
AO-38	Content of an Appraisal Report and Restricted Appraisal Report

SECTION TWO ADVISORY OPINIONS ORGANIZED BY APPRAISAL DISCIPLINE

Personal Property Advisory Opinions

AO-2	Inspection of the Property
AO-3	Update of a Prior Appraisal
AO-7	Marketing Time Opinions
AO-18	Use of an Automated Valuation Model (AVM)
AO-20	An Appraisal Review Assignment that Includes the Reviewer's Own Opinion of Value
AO-24	Normal Course of Business
AO-26	Readdressing (Transferring) a Report to Another Party
AO-27	Appraising the Same Property for a New Client
AO-28	Scope of Work Decision, Performance, and Disclosure
AO-29	An Acceptable Scope of Work
AO-31	Assignments Involving More Than One Appraiser
AO-32	Ad Valorem Property Tax Appraisal and Mass Appraisal Assignments
AO-34	Retrospective and Prospective Value Opinions
AO-35	Reasonable Exposure Time in Real and Personal Property Opinions of Value
AO-36	Identification and Disclosure of Client, Intended Use, and Intended Users
AO-38	Content of an Appraisal Report and Restricted Appraisal Report

Intangible Property Advisory Opinions (includes business interests)

AO-3	Update of a Prior Appraisal
AO-18	Use of an Automated Valuation Model (AVM)
AO-20	An Appraisal Review Assignment that Includes the Reviewer's Own Opinion of Value
AO-26	Readdressing (Transferring) a Report to Another Party
AO-27	Appraising the Same Property for a New Client
AO-29	An Acceptable Scope of Work
AO-31	Assignments Involving More Than One Appraiser
AO-36	Identification and Disclosure of Client, Intended Use, and Intended Users
AO-38	Content of an Appraisal Report and Restricted Appraisal Report

SECTION THREE

FAQ History: Identifying Numbers and Titles

SECTION THREE FAQ HISTORY: IDENTIFYING NUMBERS AND TITLES

FAQ History
Identifying Numbers and Titles

The first time the FAQs appeared in the USPAP publication was in the 2008-2009 edition. Because USPAP changes periodically, and new FAQs are added to each edition, the identifying numbers for each FAQ will change from one edition to another. The following tables provide the identifying number for all FAQs over time.

NOTE: In a few places, the FAQ number is preceded by the letter "r". This means the FAQ was renamed and given a new number. For example, when you see "r#12" as is shown here:

2008-09 FAQ #	2010-11 FAQ #	2012-13 FAQ #	2014-15 FAQ #	2016-17 FAQ #	2018-19 FAQ #	2020-22 FAQ #	USPAP COMPOSITION, STRUCTURE, AND COMPLIANCE
11	r#12						Don't Accept Unless You Can Appraise for
	12	12	10	11	10		Don't Accept Unless You Can Appraise for $XXX,000

this means the FAQ existed in the 2008-2009 edition under the name: "Don't Accept Unless You Can Appraise For," and then in 2010-2011, the FAQ not only received a new identifying number, but its name was changed to "Don't Accept Unless You Can Appraise for $XXX,000."

FAQs that appear in gray text have been removed from the 2020-2022 USPAP publication.

FAQs
USPAP COMPOSITION, STRUCTURE, AND COMPLIANCE

2008-09 FAQ #	2010-11 FAQ #	2012-13 FAQ #	2014-15 FAQ #	2016-17 FAQ #	2018-19 FAQ #	2020-22 FAQ #	USPAP COMPOSITION, STRUCTURE, AND COMPLIANCE
				1	1	1	Applicable Edition of USPAP
1	1	1	1	2			Advisory Opinions Not Part of USPAP
2	2	2	2				Valuation Service Defined
3	3	3	3	3			Retiring a Portion of USPAP
4	4	4					The Primary Intent of USPAP
5							Main Function of USPAP
6	5	5	4	4	2	2	Complying with USPAP by Choice
7	6	6					Compliance with USPAP: Personal Property, Business Valuation and Intangible Asset Appraisers
	7	7	5	5	3	3	USPAP Applicability in Valuation for Financial Reporting
	8	8	6	6	4	4	Assignment Involving Analysis of Leases
8	9	9	7	7	5	5	USPAP Compliance as an Instructor
9	10	10	8	8	6	6	Personal Property Appraisal Requirements
10	11	11	9	9	7	7	USPAP Compliance with Other Valuation Standards
				10	8	8	Differences Between Appraisal and Appraisal Report
					9	9	Public Trust

FAQs
ETHICS RULE – CONDUCT

2008-09 FAQ #	2010-11 FAQ #	2012-13 FAQ #	2014-15 FAQ #	2016-17 FAQ #	2018-19 FAQ #	2020-22 FAQ #	ETHICS RULE – CONDUCT
11	r# 12						Don't Accept Unless You Can Appraise for
	12	12	10	11	10	r# 10	Don't Accept Unless You Can Appraise for $XXX,000
						10	Don't Agree to Perform the Assignment Unless You Can Appraise for $XXX,000
	13	13	11	12	11	11	Appraiser Coercion
12	14	14	12	13	12	12	Plagiarism
13	r# 15						Subjective Terms
	15	15	13	14	13	13	Use of Qualitative Terms
14	16	16	14	15	14	14	Conflicts of Interest
		17	15	16	15	15	Disclosing Prior Appraisal of a Property
			16	17	16	16	Appraising a Property More Than Once in Three Years
		18	17	18	17	17	Disclosure Requirements When an Appraiser has Not Performed Services Regarding a Property in the Prior Three Years
		19	18	19	18	18	Disclosure of Any Prior Services Regarding the Subject Property, When an Appraiser Has Appraised the Property Multiple Times
			19	20	19	19	Disclosure of Prior Services
		20	20				Disclosing Additional Information Regarding a Prior Appraisal
		21	21				Client Requirements to Maintain Confidentiality

FAQs
ETHICS RULE – CONDUCT

2008-09 FAQ #	2010-11 FAQ #	2012-13 FAQ #	2014-15 FAQ #	2016-17 FAQ #	2018-19 FAQ #	2020-22 FAQ #	ETHICS RULE – CONDUCT
		22	22				Disclosure of Any prior services regarding the subject property before accepting an Assignment, When the Client Had Previously Required an Appraiser to Sign a Confidentiality Agreement
			23				Adding a "Disclaimer" for Disclosure of Prior Services
		23	24	21	20	20	Disclosure of Any Prior Services Regarding the Subject Property before Agreeing to Perform an Assignment, When the Appraiser Only Works for One Client
		24	25	22	21	21	Disclosure of Any Prior Services Regarding the Subject Property, When an Appraiser Has Performed Services Other Than Appraisal Practice
		25	26				Disclosing Prior Services More Than Three Years Ago
		26	27	23	22	22	Disclosing Prior Services Provided by My Company
		27	28	24	23	23	Disclosing Prospective Interest in a Property
		28	29	25	24	r# 24	Disclosing Prior Services on Pre-Printed Form Reports
						24	Disclosing Prior Services When Forms Do Not Include All of the Required Certification Elements
			30	26	25	25	Does a Request for a "Final Inspection" Require Disclosure of Prior Services?
			31	27	26	26	Does Utilizing a Property as a Comparable Sale Require Disclosure of Prior Services?
		29	32	r #28			Is There a Specified Format for Disclosing Prior Services at the Time of Assignment?
				28	27	27	Format for Disclosing Prior Services at the Time of Assignment
15	17						Using a Flawed Appraisal Report

SECTION THREE FAQ HISTORY: IDENTIFYING NUMBERS AND TITLES

FAQs
ETHICS RULE – CONDUCT

2008-09 FAQ #	2010-11 FAQ #	2012-13 FAQ #	2014-15 FAQ #	2016-17 FAQ #	2018-19 FAQ #	2020-22 FAQ #	ETHICS RULE – CONDUCT
16	18	30	33	29	28	28	Value Opinions That Equal Contract Prices
17	19	31					Property Flipping
18	20	32	34	30	29	29	Are Condition and Marketability Reports Covered by USPAP?
19	21	33	35	31			Supported and Unsupported Conclusions
20	22	34	36	32	30	30	Unacceptable Assignment Conditions-Nondisclosure of Facts
21							Things of Value Received for Procurement of an Assignment
					31	31	Does Disclosure of Prior Services Apply to Appraiser or Property?
						32	Disclosure of Prior Services Involving a Partnership
						33	Disclosure of Prior Services for Multiple Assignments on a Property

FAQs
ETHICS RULE – MANAGEMENT

2008-09 FAQ #	2010-11 FAQ #	2012-13 FAQ #	2014-15 FAQ #	2016-17 FAQ #	2018-19 FAQ #	2020-22 FAQ #	ETHICS RULE – MANAGEMENT
	23	35	37	33	32	34	Fees Paid for Procurement of an Assignment
22	24	36	38	34	33	35	Coupons for Price Discounts
23	25	37	39	35	34	36	Payment of Fees to be Included on Approved Appraisers List
24	26	38	40	36	35	37	Conducting Drawings to Procure Appraisal Assignments
25	27	39	41	37	36	38	Reducing Appraisal Fees When Transactions Fail to Close
26	28	40	42	38	37	39	Appraisal Fees as Percentages of Value Conclusions
27	29	41	43	39	38	40	Appraisal Fee is Contingent on the Appraised Value
			44	40	39	41	Appraisal Fee Based on Outcome of an Assignment
			45	41	40	42	Acting as an Appraiser
				42	41	43	"USPAP Certified" Advertisement
28	30	42	46	43	42	44	Appraiser's Fees Based on Pending Sale Price
29	r# 23						Paying Fees for Procuring Appraisal Assignments
30	r# 31						"Discounted" Appraisal Fees
	31	43	47	44	43	45	Discounted Appraisal Fees
31	r# 32						Disclosure of Referral Fees
	32	44	48	45	44	46	Disclosure of Referral Fee Amounts
32	33	45	49	46	45	47	Reciprocal Business Arrangements

SECTION THREE FAQ HISTORY: IDENTIFYING NUMBERS AND TITLES

FAQs
ETHICS RULE – MANAGEMENT

2008-09 FAQ #	2010-11 FAQ #	2012-13 FAQ #	2014-15 FAQ #	2016-17 FAQ #	2018-19 FAQ #	2020-22 FAQ #	ETHICS RULE – MANAGEMENT
33	34	46	50	47	46	48	Does USPAP Apply if There is no Assignment Fee?
	35	47	51	48	47	49	Can Appraisers Perform Comp Check Assignments for Free?
		36	48	52	49	48	50	Is Disclosure of a Free Comp Check Assignment Required?
34	37	49	53	50	49	51	Appraisal Fee Paid at Close of Financing Transaction
						52	Payment of a Portal Fee
		50	54				Collecting Fee on Behalf of an AMC

FAQs
ETHICS RULE – CONFIDENTIALITY

2008-09 FAQ #	2010-11 FAQ #	2012-13 FAQ #	2014-15 FAQ #	2016-17 FAQ #	2018-19 FAQ #	2020-22 FAQ #	ETHICS RULE – CONFIDENTIALITY
35	38	51	55	51	50	53	Reporting of Adverse Conditions
		52	56	52	51	54	Due Process of Law
36	39	53	57	53	52	55	Disclosing Results of Appraisal Assignments
				54	53	56	"Verifying" Completion of an Appraisal
	40	54	58	55	54	57	Appraisal Report Received by Others
37	41	55	59	56	55	58	Disclosure of a Prior Assignment
38	42	56	60	57			Disclosure of the Client in a Prior Assignment
	43	57	61	58			Can an Appraiser Disclose the Identity of Past Clients in an Appraisal Report?
39	44	58	62	r #59			Sample Appraisals and the Ethics Rule
				59	56	59	Sample Appraisal Reports and the Ethics Rule
	45	59	63	60	57	60	Providing Sample Appraisal Reports
40	46	60	64	61	58	61	Confidentiality and Sample Appraisal Reports
41	47	61	65	62	59	62	Delivering a Report by Email to a Client
	48	62	66	63	60	63	Confidentiality and Intended Users
	49	63	67	64	61	64	Confidentiality and Review Appraisers
42	50	r #64					Disclosure of Assignment Results to State Appraiser Board
		64	68	65	62	65	Disclosure of Assignment Results to State Appraiser Regulatory Agency

FAQs
ETHICS RULE – CONFIDENTIALITY

2008-09 FAQ #	2010-11 FAQ #	2012-13 FAQ #	2014-15 FAQ #	2016-17 FAQ #	2018-19 FAQ #	2020-22 FAQ #	ETHICS RULE – CONFIDENTIALITY
	51	65	69	66	63	66	Due Process Under Confidentiality
	52	66	70	67	64	67	Communicating Confidential Information to a Sworn Police Officer
43	53	67	71	68	65	68	Confidentiality and Peer Review Committees
44	54	68	72	69	66	69	Confidentiality and Privacy Regulations
	55	69	73	70	67	70	When Does Appraiser-Client Confidentiality End?
	56	70	74	71	68	71	Copyrighting an Appraisal Report
45	57	71	75	72	69	72	Selling an Appraisal Firm and Ethical Obligations
46	58	72	76	73	70	73	Purchasing an Appraisal Firm and Ethical Obligations
					71	74	Providing a Copy of a Workfile
					72	75	Are Physical Characteristics Confidential?
					73	76	Physical Characteristics or Assignment Results?
					74	77	Physical Characteristics or Assignment Results – Residential Real Property Example
					75	77	Physical Characteristics or Assignment Results – Non-Residential Real Property Example
					76	79	Physical Characteristics or Assignment Results – Machinery and Equipment Example
					77	80	Physical Characteristics or Assignment Results – Fine Art Example
					78	81	What are "Reasonable Steps"?

SECTION THREE FAQ HISTORY: IDENTIFYING NUMBERS AND TITLES

FAQs
RECORD KEEPING RULE

2008-09 FAQ #	2010-11 FAQ #	2012-13 FAQ #	2014-15 FAQ #	2016-17 FAQ #	2018-19 FAQ #	2020-22 FAQ #	RECORD KEEPING RULE
47	59	73	77	74	79	82	Contents of a Workfile
48	60	74					Time Period to Retain Workfiles
		75	78	75	80	83	Disposal of Workfiles
49	61	76	79	76	81	84	Photocopies of Appraisal Reports in Workfiles
50	62	77	80	77	82	85	Workfiles for Appraisal Review Assignments
51	63	78	81	78	83	86	Purging Workfiles at a Client's Request
52	64	79	82	79	84	87	Workfile Retention with More Than One Appraiser
53	65	80	83	80	85	88	Responsibility for Workfile Retention
54	66	81	84	81	86	89	Trainee Access to Workfiles
	67	82	85	82	87	90	Appropriate Workfile Retention and Access Arrangements
	68	83	86	83	88	91	May Access to a Workfile be Denied?
		84	87	84	89	92	Access and Retrieval of Workfiles
55	69	85	88	85	90	93	Signed Certification in True Copies
56	70	86	89	86	91	94	Creating a Workfile After Report Delivery
	71	87	90	87	92	95	Is a Transcript Required for Oral Report and Testimony?
	72	88	91	88	93	96	Is a Transcript Required if a Written Appraisal Report Was Prepared?
	73	89	92	89	94	97	Record Keeping Requirements for Oral Reports and Testimony

SECTION THREE FAQ HISTORY: IDENTIFYING NUMBERS AND TITLES

FAQs
RECORD KEEPING RULE

2008-09 FAQ #	2010-11 FAQ #	2012-13 FAQ #	2014-15 FAQ #	2016-17 FAQ #	2018-19 FAQ #	2020-22 FAQ #	RECORD KEEPING RULE
	74	90	93	90	95	98	Is a Separate Certification Required if a Written Appraisal Report Was Prepared?
	75	91	94	91	96	99	Is a Transcript of the Entire Proceeding Required?
57	76	92	95	92	97	100	Electronic Workfile Storage
58	77	93					Paper Copies of Electronically Transmitted Reports
	78	94	96	93	98	101	Adequacy of Workfile Documentation
59	79	95	97	94	99	102	Jurisdictional Exception and Workfile Retention
60	80	96	98	95	100	103	Minimum Workfile Retention
						104	Workfile Requirements When Communicating Assignment Results
						105	Workfiles Affected by a National Disaster
						106	Appraising After a Natural Disaster
						107	Maintaining Records for a Deceased Appraiser
						108	Government Agency Workfile Retention
						109	Testimony and Deposition
						110	Retention Requirements for Preliminary Communications After Completion of the Assignment

FAQs
COMPETENCY RULE

2008-09 FAQ #	2010-11 FAQ #	2012-13 FAQ #	2014-15 FAQ #	2016-17 FAQ #	2018-19 FAQ #	2020-22 FAQ #	COMPETENCY RULE
61	81	97	99	96	101	111	Acquiring Knowledge & Experience to Comply with the Competency Rule
		98	100	97	102	112	Assignment Conditions, Scope of Work Acceptability and Geographic Competency
62	82	99	101	98	103	113	Continuing Education Courses
	83	100	102	99	104	114	Competency Statement in the Report
	84	101	103	100	105	115	Errors and Omissions Insurance

SECTION THREE FAQ HISTORY: IDENTIFYING NUMBERS AND TITLES

FAQs
JURISDICTIONAL EXCEPTION RULE

2008-09 FAQ #	2010-11 FAQ #	2012-13 FAQ #	2014-15 FAQ #	2016-17 FAQ #	2018-19 FAQ #	2020-22 FAQ #	JURISDICTIONAL EXCEPTION RULE
63	85	102	104	101	106	116	Application of the JURISDICTIONAL EXCEPTION RULE
64	86	103	105	102	107	117	USPAP Compliance and Jurisdictional Exception
65	r #87						When USPAP is Contrary to Public Policy or Law
	87	104	106	103	108	118	When Compliance with USPAP is Precluded by Law or Regulation
	88	105	107	104	109	119	Probate Court Statute Basing the Appraisal Fee on the Appraised Value
66	89	106	108	105	110	120	Appropriate Sources for Jurisdictional Exception
	90	107	109	106	111	121	Valuation Methods and Jurisdictional Exception Rule
		108	110	107	112	122	Client Requirement to Disregard Market Value Changes Prior to Effective Date
		109	111	108	R# 113		Client Requirement to Disregard the Influence on Market Value of Public Improvements
					113	123	Client Requirement to Disregard Linking Opinion of Value to a Specific Exposure Time
		110	112	109	114	124	Is a "Waiver Valuation" a Jurisdictional Exception?
		111	113	110	115	125	Client Requirement to Assume No Contamination Exists
67	91	112	114	111	116	126	Jurisdictional Exception and Confidentiality

FAQs
APPRAISAL DEVELOPMENT – CLIENT ISSUES

2008-09 FAQ #	2010-11 FAQ #	2012-13 FAQ #	2014-15 FAQ #	2016-17 FAQ #	2018-19 FAQ #	2020-22 FAQ #	APPRAISAL DEVELOPMENT – CLIENT ISSUES
68	92	113					Identification of the Client
69	93	114	115	112	117	127	Payment by a Party Other Than the Client
70	94	115	116	113	118	128	Difference Between Clients and Intended Users
71	95	116	117	114	119	129	Appraisal Management Company as Authorized Agent for a Client
		117	118	115	120	130	Can an Appraisal Management Company be the Client?
72	96	118	119	116	121	131	Client Cannot be Identified
73	r #97						Subsequent User Requests a "Reliance Letter"
73	97	119	120	117	122	132	Subsequent User Requests a Reliance Letter
74	98	120	121	118	123	133	Readdress or Transfer
75	99	121	122	119	124	134	Readdressing with Lender Release
76	100	122	123	120	125	135	Identification of Intended Users
	101	123	124	121	126	136	Addresses, Clients, and Intended Users
	102	124	125	122	127	137	Appraising Without Knowing the Intended Use or Intended User
77	103	125	126	123	128	138	Are Borrowers Intended Users?
78	104	126	127	124	129	139	Identifying Intended Users by Type
79	105	127	128	125	130	140	Engaged Directly by the Homeowner
80	106	128	129	126	131	141	Client Approval for Future Assignments
		129	130	127	132	142	Request to Modify a Completed Appraisal Report

FAQs
APPRAISAL DEVELOPMENT – CLIENT ISSUES

2008-09 FAQ #	2010-11 FAQ #	2012-13 FAQ #	2014-15 FAQ #	2016-17 FAQ #	2018-19 FAQ #	2020-22 FAQ #	APPRAISAL DEVELOPMENT – CLIENT ISSUES
				128	133	143	Shelf Life of an Appraisal or Appraisal Report
			131	129	134	144	Use of Distress Sales in Real Property Market Value Appraisals
						145	Adding an Intended User
						146	Assignment Conditions Versus Client Conditions

SECTION THREE FAQ HISTORY: IDENTIFYING NUMBERS AND TITLES

FAQs
APPRAISAL DEVELOPMENT – APPRAISAL DATES

2008-09 FAQ #	2010-11 FAQ #	2012-13 FAQ #	2014-15 FAQ #	2016-17 FAQ #	2018-19 FAQ #	2020-22 FAQ #	APPRAISAL DEVELOPMENT – APPRAISAL DATES
81	107	130	132	130	135	147	Effective Date of the Appraisal
82	108	131	133	131			Date of Appraisal
83	109	132	134	132			Date of Value
					136	148	Appraisal Dates
	110	133	135	133	137	149	Citation of Effective Date
	111	134	136	134	138	150	Changing the Effective Date
			137	135	139	151	Date of Report
			138	136	140	152	Date of Revised Report
	112	135	139	137			Does Changing the Sale Price Result in a New Assignment?
					141	153	Revision to the Contract Price
84	113	136					Current Value Opinions for Proposed Improvements
85	114	137	140	138	142	154	Proposed Improvements- Current and Prospective Value Opinions
		138	141	139	143	155	Effective Date and Date of the Report
86	115	139	142	140	144	156	Competency as of Effective Date of the Appraisal
87	116	140	143	141	145	157	Current and Retrospective Value Opinion Within One Report
88	117	141	144	142	146	158	Post-Value Date Information in Retrospective Appraisals

SECTION THREE FAQ HISTORY: IDENTIFYING NUMBERS AND TITLES

FAQs
APPRAISAL DEVELOPMENT – APPRAISAL DATES

2008-09 FAQ #	2010-11 FAQ #	2012-13 FAQ #	2014-15 FAQ #	2016-17 FAQ #	2018-19 FAQ #	2020-22 FAQ #	**APPRAISAL DEVELOPMENT – APPRAISAL DATES**
89	118	142	145	143	147	159	Appraisal Based on Current and Prospective Date of Value
90	119	143	146	144	148	160	USPAP Compliance in Retrospective Appraisals
91	120	144	147	145	149	161	Retrospective Appraisal Assignments
132	r# 179						Citing the Source of the Value Definition and Fannie Mae Form 1004
	179	203	148	146	150	162	Citing the Source of the Value Definition and Fannie Mae Form 1004/Freddie Mac Form 70

FAQs
APPRAISAL DEVELOPMENT – SCOPE OF WORK ISSUES

2008-09 FAQ #	2010-11 FAQ #	2012-13 FAQ #	2014-15 FAQ #	2016-17 FAQ #	2018-19 FAQ #	2020-22 FAQ #	APPRAISAL DEVELOPMENT – SCOPE OF WORK ISSUES
92	121	145	149	147	151	163	What is Scope of Work?
93	122	146	150	148	152	164	Applicability of Scope of Work Rule
94	123	147	151	148	153	165	Responsibility for the Scope of Work Decision
95	124	148	152	150	154	166	Client Specifies Scope of Work
			153	151	155	167	Alternative Valuation Products
		149	154	152	156	168	Client Request to Limit Scope of Work to New Client Name
	125	150	155	153	157	169	The Impact of Different Clients on Assignment Results with Otherwise Identical Assignment Elements and Scope of Work
	126	151					Obligation to Analyze Withdrawn or Expired Listings
96	r #127						How "Credible" Results are Measured
	127	152	156	154	158	170	How Credible Assignment Results are Measured
	128	153	157	155	159	171	Errors of Commission and Omission
	129	154	158	156	160	172	Making a Series of Errors
	130	155	159	157	161	173	Changing the Scope of Work After the Report Has Been Submitted
97							Standards, Standards Rules, and Developing an Appraisal
98	r #131						Judging an "Appraiser's Peer Actions"

SECTION THREE FAQ HISTORY: IDENTIFYING NUMBERS AND TITLES

FAQs
APPRAISAL DEVELOPMENT – SCOPE OF WORK ISSUES

2008-09 FAQ #	2010-11 FAQ #	2012-13 FAQ #	2014-15 FAQ #	2016-17 FAQ #	2018-19 FAQ #	2020-22 FAQ #	APPRAISAL DEVELOPMENT – SCOPE OF WORK ISSUES
				158	162	174	Differing Scopes of Work
	131	156	160	159	163	175	Judging the Actions of an Appraiser's Peers
99	132	157	161	160	164	176	Type and Definition of Value, and Citation of Source
	133	158	162	161	165	177	Market Rent Opinion
100	134	159	163	162	166	178	Using the Definition of Value Provided
	135	160	164	163	167	179	Sales or Financing Concessions
	136	161	165	164	168	180	Intentionally Deflating Opinions of Value
101	137	162	166	165	169	181	Measuring Single Family Residences using the ANSI Standard
102	138	163	167	166	170	182	Exposure Time and Marketing Time
			168	167	171	183	Marketing Time on Appraisal Forms
			169	168	172	184	Exposure Time Value Range
103	139						Analyzing and Reporting of Exposure Time
	140	164	170	169	173	185	Checking Stable vs. Declining Property Values
104	141	165	171	170	174	186	Range of Value
105	142	166	172	171	175	187	More Than One Intended Use
106	142	167	173	172	176	188	Value in Use Request from Federally Regulated Lender
107	144	168	174	173	177	189	Drive-by and Desktop Appraisals

FAQs
APPRAISAL DEVELOPMENT – SCOPE OF WORK ISSUES

2008-09 FAQ #	2010-11 FAQ #	2012-13 FAQ #	2014-15 FAQ #	2016-17 FAQ #	2018-19 FAQ #	2020-22 FAQ #	APPRAISAL DEVELOPMENT – SCOPE OF WORK ISSUES
108	145	169	175	174	178	190	Inspection of Subject Property
	146	170	176	175	179	191	Does Inspecting Photographs Constitute a Personal Inspection of a Subject Property?
	147	171	177	176	180	192	Is it Permissible to Use MLS Photos for Comparable Sales?
	148	172	178	177	181	193	Is it Permissible to Use MLS Photos for Active Listings?
109	149	173	179	178	182	r# 194	Cost Approach not Necessary for Appraisal of Vacant Land
						194	Is the Cost Approach Necessary for Appraisal of Vacant Land?
110	r #150						Cost Approach and Fannie Mae Form 1004
	150	174	180	179			Cost Approach and Fannie Mae Form 1004/Freddie Mac Form 70
111	151	175	181	180			Appraising Improved Land
112	152	176	182	181	183	195	Improvement Only Appraisal
113	153	177	183	182	184	196	Appraising Only the Underlying Land of an Improved Property
114	154	178	184	183	185	197	Appraising Physical Segments (5-Acre Portion)
	155	179					Income and Expense Analyses
115	156	180	185	184	186	198	Proposed Improvements-Plans and Specifications Required
	157	181	186	185	187	199	Is an AVM an Appraisal?
	158	182	187	186	188	200	Appraiser's USPAP Obligations When Using an AVM

SECTION THREE FAQ HISTORY: IDENTIFYING NUMBERS AND TITLES

FAQs
APPRAISAL DEVELOPMENT – SCOPE OF WORK ISSUES

2008-09 FAQ #	2010-11 FAQ #	2012-13 FAQ #	2014-15 FAQ #	2016-17 FAQ #	2018-19 FAQ #	2020-22 FAQ #	APPRAISAL DEVELOPMENT – SCOPE OF WORK ISSUES
	159	183	188	187	189	201	Uniform Act and Scope of Work
116	160	184	189	188	190	202	Appraising Large Groups of Similar or Like Items
117	161	185	190	189	r# 191		Blockage Discount and Standard 6
					191	203	Blockage Discount and Standard 5
118	162	186	191	190	192	204	Calculating Blockage Discount
119	163	187	192	191	193	205	Business Valuation Using Asset-Based (Cost) Approach
	164	188	193	192	194	206	Allocation of Value Opinions
120	165	189	194	193	195	207	Leased Fee Interest When Intangible Assets Exist
121	166	190	195	194	196	208	Purchase Contract is not Provided to the Appraiser
122	167	191	196	195	197	209	Availability of Current Agreement of Sale
123	168	192	197	196	198	210	Reconciliation of the Approaches to Value
124	169	193	198	197	199	211	Adjustments in Sales Comparison Approach
125	170	194	199	198	200	212	Updating a Prior Assignment with a Different Scope of Work
	171	195	200	199	201	213	Appraisal Update with No Change in Value
126	172	196	201	200	202	214	Update of an Appraisal Completed by Another Appraiser
127	173	197	202	201	203	215	Does a New Assignment Require Starting Over?
128	174	198	203	202	204	216	Recertification of Value

FAQs
APPRAISAL DEVELOPMENT – SCOPE OF WORK ISSUES

2008-09 FAQ #	2010-11 FAQ #	2012-13 FAQ #	2014-15 FAQ #	2016-17 FAQ #	2018-19 FAQ #	2020-22 FAQ #	APPRAISAL DEVELOPMENT – SCOPE OF WORK ISSUES
129	175	199	204	203	205	217	Recertification of Value and Appraisal Update
130	r #176						Appraisers "Providing Comps"
	176	200	205	204	206	218	Appraisers Providing Comps
	177	201	206	205	207	219	Can Appraisers Perform Comp Check Assignments?
131	178	202	207	206	208	220	Sudden Market Changes Related to Catastrophic Events
			208	207	209	r# 221	Encumbrances on Personal Property
						221	Restrictions or Encumbrances on Personal Property
			209	208	210	222	Liens on Personal Property
					211	223	Appraising Two Lots as One
					212	224	Impact on Values of Surrounding Properties
					213	225	Is Turnaround Time an Assignment Condition
					214	226	Inspection Using a Drone
						227	Can I Perform an Appraisal if the Property Inspection Was Done by Someone Else?
						228	Analyzing the Subject's Operating History
						229	Personal Inspection Timing
						230	Intangible Personal Property
						231	Appraising Large Quantities – Not Necessarily a Mass Appraisal

FAQs
APPRAISAL DEVELOPMENT – EXTRAORDINARY ASSUMPTIONS AND HYPOTHETICAL CONDITIONS

2008-09 FAQ #	2010-11 FAQ #	2012-13 FAQ #	2014-15 FAQ #	2016-17 FAQ #	2018-19 FAQ #	2020-22 FAQ #	APPRAISAL DEVELOPMENT – EXTRAORDINARY ASSUMPTIONS AND HYPOTHETICAL CONDITIONS
133	180	204	210	209	215	232	Extraordinary Assumptions Compared to Hypothetical Conditions
134	181	205	211	210	216	233	Hypothetical Conditions Described
135	182	206	211	211	217	234	When a Hypothetical Condition May be Used
	183	207	213	212	218	235	Before Acquisition Value and Standards Rule 1-4(f)
136	184	208	214	213	219	236	Reporting Use of Extraordinary Assumptions and Hypothetical Conditions
	185	209	215	214	220	237	Must a Hypothetical Condition or Extraordinary Assumption Be Labeled?
137	186	210	216	215	221	238	Value as if Completed
138	r#187						Appraising a Property not in "As Is" Condition
	187	211	217	216	222	239	Appraising a Property not in As-Is Condition
139	188	212	218	217	223	240	Analyzing the Lease When Appraising Fee Simple Interest
140	189	213	219	218	224	241	Definition of Extraordinary Assumption
						242	Proposed Construction Employing an Extraordinary Assumption
						243	Employing an Extraordinary Assumption when a Client Provides Inspection Data
						244	Can an Extraordinary Assumption be Used without a Reasonable Basis?

SECTION THREE FAQ HISTORY: IDENTIFYING NUMBERS AND TITLES

FAQs
APPRAISAL DEVELOPMENT – SUBJECT PROPERTY SALES HISTORY

2008-09 FAQ #	2010-11 FAQ #	2012-13 FAQ #	2014-15 FAQ #	2016-17 FAQ #	2018-19 FAQ #	2020-22 FAQ #	APPRAISAL DEVELOPMENT – SUBJECT PROPERTY SALES HISTORY
141							USPAP Requirements for Analyzing Prior Sales of Subject Property
142	190	214	220	219	225	245	Multiple Sales or Transfers of the Subject Property
143	191	215	221	220	226	246	Offers to Purchase Subject Property
	192	216	222	221	227	247	Current Sales Contract Is Not Provided
144	193	217	223	222	228	248	Pending Sales as Comparables
145	194	218					Subject Property Sales History and Property Flipping
146	195	219	224	223	229	249	Subject Property as a Comparable Sale
147	196	220	225	224	230	250	Five-Year Sales History as an Assignment Condition
148	197	221					Analysis of Subject Property Sales History
	198	222	226	225	231	251	Sales History for New Construction
	199	223	227	226	232	252	Appraisal Without Knowing Sale Price
149	200	224	228	227	233	253	Analysis of Sales History for Comparable Sales
150	201	225	229	228	234	254	Sales History Analysis for Deed in Lieu of Foreclosure
151	202	226	230	229	235	255	Obligation to Analyze Prior Listings of Subject Property
	203	227	231	230	236	256	Proper Analysis of Agreement of Sale
				231	237	257	Value Conclusion Below Contract Price

FAQs
APPRAISAL DEVELOPMENT – SUBJECT PROPERTY SALES HISTORY

2008-09 FAQ #	2010-11 FAQ #	2012-13 FAQ #	2014-15 FAQ #	2016-17 FAQ #	2018-19 FAQ #	2020-22 FAQ #	APPRAISAL DEVELOPMENT – SUBJECT PROPERTY SALES HISTORY
152	r# 126						Obligation to Analyze Withdrawn or Expired Listings
	204	228	232	232	238	258	Obligation to Analyze Withdrawn or Expired Listings
153	205	229	233	233	239	259	Sales History Analysis in a Retrospective Appraisal
154	r #206						Sales History Analysis for "Condition and Marketability" Reports
	206	230	234	234	240	260	Sales History Analysis for Condition and Marketability Reports
					241	261	Subject Property Sales History and Standards Rule 1-5(b)
						262	Sales History in Machinery and Equipment Appraisal Assignment
						263	Sales History in Fine and Decorative Arts Appraisal Assignment
						264	Changes in Composition of Partnerships or Corporations

FAQs
APPRAISAL REPORTING – CERTIFICATION AND SIGNATURES

2008-09 FAQ #	2010-11 FAQ #	2012-13 FAQ #	2014-15 FAQ #	2016-17 FAQ #	2018-19 FAQ #	2020-22 FAQ #	APPRAISAL REPORTING – CERTIFICATION AND SIGNATURES
155	207	231	235	235	242	265	Reason for Signed Certification
				236	243	266	Use of Certification with Form 1004D/442
	208	232	236	237	244	267	Changing the Certification
			237	238	245	r# 268	Revising Pre-Printed Certification to Disclose Prior Services
						268	Revising Appraisal Form Certification to Disclose Prior Services
	209	233	238	239	246	269	Requirement for Signing Reports
	210	234	239	240	247	270	Signature on Letter of Transmittal
156	211	235	240	241	248	271	Multiple Signatures on Appraisal Reports
157	212	236	241	242	249	272	Signature Authorization
	213	237					Authorizing the Use of Your Digital Signature
	214	238	242	243	250	273	Providing Signature to Create a Signature File
	215	239	243	244	251	274	Losing Control of a Digital Signature
	216	240	244	245	252	275	Responsibility of an Appraiser Signing as a Supervisor
158	r #216						Responsibility of an Appraiser Signing as a "Supervisor"
	217	241	245	246	253	276	Signing Digital (Electronic) Reports
159	218	242	246	247	254	277	Business Entity Signing an Appraisal Report
	219	243	247	248	255	278	Significant Appraisal Assistance

FAQs
APPRAISAL REPORTING – CERTIFICATION AND SIGNATURES

2008-09 FAQ #	2010-11 FAQ #	2012-13 FAQ #	2014-15 FAQ #	2016-17 FAQ #	2018-19 FAQ #	2020-22 FAQ #	APPRAISAL REPORTING – CERTIFICATION AND SIGNATURES
				249	256	279	Utilizing a Data Entry Service
		244	248	250	257	r# 280	Significant Professional Assistance
						280	Have I Provided Significant Appraisal Assistance?
			249	251	258	281	Reporting Significant Appraisal Assistance in an Oral Report
160	220	245	250	252	259	282	Does USPAP Define Supervisory Appraiser?
161	221	246	251	253	260	283	Reporting Significant Real Property Appraisal Assistance
			252	254	261	284	Relying on the Reports of Others
162	222	248	253	255	262	285	Disagree with Supervisor on Value Conclusion
	223	249	254	256	263	286	Does the Certification on a Uniform Residential Appraisal Report (URAR) Form Also Extend to the Market Conditions Addendum?
163	224	250	255	257	264	287	Multi-Discipline Certification - Real Property Appraiser
164	225	251	256				Relying on the Reports of Others
165	226	252					Multi-Discipline Certification - Personal Property Appraiser
			257	258	265	288	Significant Appraisal Assistance - Personal Property Appraiser
					266	289	Use of Certification with Form 1004D/442 - Appraisal Update
					267	290	Use of Certification with Form 1004D/442 - Satisfactory Completion

FAQs
APPRAISAL REPORTING – CERTIFICATION AND SIGNATURES

2008-09 FAQ #	2010-11 FAQ #	2012-13 FAQ #	2014-15 FAQ #	2016-17 FAQ #	2018-19 FAQ #	2020-22 FAQ #	APPRAISAL REPORTING – CERTIFICATION AND SIGNATURES
					268	291	Certification with Multiple Appraisers
						292	Personal Property Appraisal Assignment Involving Multiple Appraisers
						293	Does USPAP Require Disclosure of Assistance by a Non-Appraiser?
						294	Signing and Labeling of Supplemental Certifications
						295	Labeling Supplemental Certifications
						296	Prior Service and Professional Assistance Disclosures (Part 1)
						297	Prior Service and Professional Assistance Disclosures (Part 2)

SECTION THREE FAQ HISTORY: IDENTIFYING NUMBERS AND TITLES

FAQs
APPRAISAL REPORTING – USE AND FORMAT ISSUES

2008-09 FAQ #	2010-11 FAQ #	2012-13 FAQ #	2014-15 FAQ #	2016-17 FAQ #	2018-19 FAQ #	2020-22 FAQ #	APPRAISAL REPORTING – USE AND FORMAT ISSUES
166	227	253					Required Level of Detail in a Self-Contained Appraisal Report
167	228	254	258	259	269	298	Ownership of Appraisal Reports
	229	255	259	260	270	299	Electronic Report Delivery
168	230	256					Identification of Report Option Used
	231	257					Appraisal Report Labeling Confusion
169	232	258	260	261	271	300	Label Different from Reporting Options
				262	272	301	Fannie Mae Form 1004
	233	259	261	263	273	302	Is a Letter of Transmittal Part of an Appraisal Report?
	234	260	262	264	274	303	Copy of License in Appraisal Report
	235	261	263	265	275	304	Does USPAP Require Identifying Appraisal Credentials?
170	236	262	264	266	276	305	Restricted Appraisal Report and Third Parties
171	237	263					Appraisal Update Reporting Format
	238	264	265	267	277	306	Are Instant Messages or Text Messages Appraisal Reports?
172	239	265	266	268	278	307	Reporting Appraisal Updates
173	r #240						Fannie Mae Update Report Form 1004D

SECTION THREE FAQ HISTORY: IDENTIFYING NUMBERS AND TITLES

FAQs
APPRAISAL REPORTING – USE AND FORMAT ISSUES

2008-09 FAQ #	2010-11 FAQ #	2012-13 FAQ #	2014-15 FAQ #	2016-17 FAQ #	2018-19 FAQ #	2020-22 FAQ #	APPRAISAL REPORTING – USE AND FORMAT ISSUES
	240	266	267	269	279	308	Fannie Mae Update Report Form 1004D/Freddie Mac Form 442
174	241	267					Appraisal Report Content and Property Flipping
175	242	268	268	270	280	309	Legal Description
176	243	269	269	271	281	310	Property Address
177	244	270	270	272	282	311	Why Report Scope of Work?
178	245	271	271	273	283	312	Reporting Work Not Done in an Assignment
				274	284	313	Explaining the Exclusion of Approaches
179	246	272	272	275	285	314	Separate Scope of Work Section in the Report
180	247	273	273	276	286	315	Identification of Intended Users in Appraisal Reports
181	248	274	274	277	287	316	Identification of Client in Appraisal Reports
182	249	275	275	278	288	317	Disclosure of the Intended User in a Report
183	250	276	276	279	289	318	Disclosure of the Intended Use in a Report
		277	277	280	290	319	Multiple Intended Uses in the Same Appraisal Report
184	251	278	278	281	291	320	Oral Reports and Record Keeping
185							Oral Appraisal Review Reporting Requirements
	252	279					Communicating Assignment Results Without a Written Report
	253	280	279	282	292	321	Oral Appraisal Reporting Requirements

SECTION THREE FAQ HISTORY: IDENTIFYING NUMBERS AND TITLES

FAQs
APPRAISAL REPORTING – USE AND FORMAT ISSUES

2008-09 FAQ #	2010-11 FAQ #	2012-13 FAQ #	2014-15 FAQ #	2016-17 FAQ #	2018-19 FAQ #	2020-22 FAQ #	APPRAISAL REPORTING – USE AND FORMAT ISSUES
186	254	281	280				Workfile Contents for an Oral Report
187	255	282	281	283	293	322	Appraisal Report Form Software
188	256	283	282	284	294	323	Paper Copies of Electronically Transmitted Reports
189	257	284	283	285	295	324	Appraisal Report Forms Compliance with USPAP
190	r #258						Fannie Mae Appraisal Report Forms and USPAP Compliance
	258	285	284	286	296		Fannie Mae/Freddie Mac Appraisal Report Forms and USPAP Compliance
191	259	286					Standards, Standards Rules and Reporting an Appraisal
		287	285	287	297	325	Application of Appraisal Reporting Requirements
192	260	288	286	288	298	326	Discounted Cash Flow (DCF)
193	r #252						Communicating Assignment Results Without a Written Report
194	r #253						Oral Appraisal Reporting Requirements
195	261	289	287	289	299	327	Content of Restricted Appraisal Reports
	262	290	288	290	300	328	Appraiser Qualifications in Report
196	263	291	289	291	301	329	Providing a Draft of a Report
197	r #264						Developing "Unnecessary" Approach
	264	292	290	292	302	330	Developing an Unnecessary Valuation Approach
			291	293	303	331	Altering Appraisal Report Photographs

FAQs
APPRAISAL REPORTING – USE AND FORMAT ISSUES

2008-09 FAQ #	2010-11 FAQ #	2012-13 FAQ #	2014-15 FAQ #	2016-17 FAQ #	2018-19 FAQ #	2020-22 FAQ #	**APPRAISAL REPORTING – USE AND FORMAT ISSUES**
					304	332	Restricted Appraisal Report for Multiple Parties
						333	Communicating Assignment Results Without an Appraisal Report
						334	Identifying Intended Users by Name in a Restricted Appraisal Report

SECTION THREE FAQ HISTORY: IDENTIFYING NUMBERS AND TITLES

FAQs
APPRAISAL REVIEW

2008-09 FAQ #	2010-11 FAQ #	2012-13 FAQ #	2014-15 FAQ #	2016-17 FAQ #	2018-19 FAQ #	2020-22 FAQ #	APPRAISAL REVIEW
198	265	293	292	294	r# 305		When Does Standard 3 Apply?
					305	335	When do Standards 3 and 4 Apply?
	266	294	293	295	306	336	Geographic Competency in Appraisal Reviews
199	267	295	294	296	307	337	Post-Valuation Date Information in Appraisal Reviews
200	268	296	295	297	308	338	Reviewer Disagrees with Value Conclusion
201	269	297	296	298	309	339	Reviewer Concurs with Value Conclusion
202	270	298	297	299	310	340	Appraisal Review and State Appraiser Boards
203	271	299	298	300	311	341	Reading Appraisal Reports
204	272	300	299	301	312	342	Reviewing Two Appraisals on the Same Property
	273	301					Must a Review Appraiser Be Licensed or Certified in the State Jurisdiction Where the Subject Property is Located
	274	302	300	302	313	343	Review Report on Multiple Appraisal Reports
205							Review Report on Three Appraisal Reports
206	275	303	301	303	314	344	Appraisal Review for a State Appraiser Board
207	276	304	302	304	315	345	Reviewing an Appraisal Review Report
208	277	305	303	305	316	346	Scope of Work in Appraisal Review Reports
209							Inspection of Subject Property

FAQs
APPRAISAL REVIEW

2008-09 FAQ #	2010-11 FAQ #	2012-13 FAQ #	2014-15 FAQ #	2016-17 FAQ #	2018-19 FAQ #	2020-22 FAQ #	APPRAISAL REVIEW
210	278	306	304	306	317	347	Reviewing a Portion of an Appraisal Report
211	279	307	305	307	318	348	Changing the Value Opinion Without the Appraiser's Consent
212	280	308	306	308	319	349	Reviewer's Own Opinion of Value and Scope of Work
213	281	309	307	309	320	350	Discrediting the Original Appraiser's Work
	282	310	308	310	321	351	Reviewer Citation of USPAP Non-Compliance
214	283	311	309	311	322	352	Review Appraiser Bias
				312	323	353	"Rebuttals" and Appraisal Reviews
	284	312	310	313	r# 324		Is Compliance with Standard 3 Required When Submitting a Complaint?
					324	354	Is Compliance with Standards 3 and 4 Required When Submitting a Complaint?
	285	313	311	314	325	355	Uniform Act and the Review of Low Value Acquisition Appraisal Reports
215	286	314	312	315	326	356	Effective Date that Differs from the Work Under Review
216	287	315	313	316	327	357	Additional Certification in an Appraisal Review Report
					328	358	Review for an Ethics Committee
					329	359	Definition of Value in Appraisal Review Reports
						360	Reviewer Highlighting the Positive
						361	Client Requirements as an Assignment Element

SECTION THREE FAQ HISTORY: IDENTIFYING NUMBERS AND TITLES

FAQs
APPRAISAL REVIEW

2008-09 FAQ #	2010-11 FAQ #	2012-13 FAQ #	2014-15 FAQ #	2016-17 FAQ #	2018-19 FAQ #	2020-22 FAQ #	APPRAISAL REVIEW
						361	Reviewer Providing Adjustments
						363	May Reviewer Say an Appraisal Lacks Analysis?
						364	Developing an Opinion of Reasonable Exposure Time

FAQs
OTHER SERVICES

2008-09 FAQ #	2010-11 FAQ #	2012-13 FAQ #	2014-15 FAQ #	2016-17 FAQ #	2018-19 FAQ #	2020-22 FAQ #	OTHER SERVICES
217	288	316					Value Opinion in an Appraisal Consulting Assignment
218	289	317	314	317	330	365	Valuation Service Involving Advocacy
219	290	318					Purpose of an Appraisal Consulting Assignment
220	291	318	315	318	331	366	Feasibility Studies and Appraisal Practice
	293	320					Appraisal Versus Appraisal Consulting Assignment
	293	321					Which USPAP Standards Apply to Personal Property Appraisal Consulting?
			316	319	332	367	Replacement Cost Estimate